The People's Bible

JOHN A. BRAUN
General Editor

ARMIN J. PANNING
New Testament Editor

ROBERT J. KOESTER
Manuscript Editor

Revelation

WAYNE D. MUELLER

NORTHWESTERN PUBLISHING HOUSE
Milwaukee, Wisconsin

Second printing, 1998

The cover and interior illustrations were originally executed by James Tissot (1836–1902).

The map on page vi was prepared by Dr. John C. Lawrenz.

Library of Congress Card 96-72092
Northwestern Publishing House
1250 N. 113th St., Milwaukee, WI 53226-3284
© 1996 by Northwestern Publishing House.
Published 1996
Printed in the United States of America
ISBN 0-8100-0674-X

CONTENTS

ILLUSTRATIONS

MAP

EDITOR'S PREFACE

The People's Bible is just what the name implies—a Bible for the people. It includes the complete text of the Holy Scriptures in the popular New International Version. The commentary following the Scripture sections contains personal applications as well as historical background and explanations of the text.

The authors of The People's Bible are men of scholarship and practical insight, gained from years of experience in the teaching and preaching ministries. They have tried to avoid the technical jargon which limits so many commentary series to professional Bible scholars.

The most important feature of these books is that they are Christ-centered. Speaking of the Old Testament Scriptures, Jesus himself declared, "These are the Scriptures that testify about me" (John 5:39). Each volume of The People's Bible directs our attention to Jesus Christ. He is the center of the entire Bible. He is our only Savior.

The commentaries also have maps, illustrations, and archaeological information when appropriate. All the books include running heads to direct the reader to the passage he is looking for.

This commentary series was initiated by the Commission on Christian Literature of the Wisconsin Evangelical Lutheran Synod.

We dedicate these volumes to the glory of God and to the good of his people.

The Seven Churches of Asia Minor

INTRODUCTION TO REVELATION

Perhaps because its title promises to uncover something new and different, the book of Revelation has always intrigued Bible students. The last book of the New Testament does, in fact, add something to the Bible's message. It provides the suffering church a beautiful new assurance of Jesus' final victory. Revelation is an expansion of the risen and ascended Savior's promise "Surely I am with you always, to the very end of the age" (Matthew 28:20).

At the heart of Revelation, however, is the same message all Scripture proclaims. Revelation centers on Jesus and his defeat of sin, death, and the devil.

Revelation differs from most of Scripture only in the way it presents its message. It is written in the style of apocalypse. *Apocalypse* is another way to translate the Bible's word for revelation. In the Bible's apocalyptic writings God inspired his prophets to use exciting word pictures to reveal what he promises for his people's future. Apocalypse, then, is bold, picturesque language that describes the coming of Jesus, either his first coming to redeem his people or his final coming to take them home.

In the Revelation this striking picture language appears in seven visions. Jesus gave John these visions to describe the New Testament age, the end of the world, judgment day, and eternity. The apocalyptic writing in these seven visions resembles the bold imagery used by Ezekiel, Daniel, Zechariah, and other Old Testament prophets. With broad strokes, Revelation paints God's picture of the church's struggles in the troubled end times and Jesus' final victory for his people.

Author, Place, Date

Revelation is one of five New Testament books written by John. The author identifies himself as John in the first and last chapters. John says that he is writing from exile on the isle of Patmos in the Aegean Sea. He was exiled there because of his testimony to Jesus. John wrote Revelation in the mid-90s of the first century after Christ. His references to suffering Christians correspond to the persecution that took place during those years under the Roman emperor Domitian.

Interpreting Revelation

Many false teachers use Revelation as a source for some strange ideas about the last days. One such misinterpretation is the millennium, supposedly a thousand-year reign by Christ on earth immediately before or after his return. There are other false notions too, such as forced mass conversions and raptures by which God snatches the faithful into heaven. To avoid drawing more or less from Revelation than God intended, it is necessary to look at how we interpret all the Bible before studying its last book.

We interpret all the Bible as God's Word. Since all Scripture has one divine source, we know that all parts of it are in perfect agreement. We also study the Revelation with the trust that it agrees with all the Bible. Although John never directly quotes Scripture, he incorporates more than five hundred scriptural paraphrases and allusions into his visions. So the Revelation stands alongside—not apart from or above—the rest of Scripture. As we begin studying it, we can be sure that this book will not introduce teachings that are foreign to the rest of God's Word.

Because the Bible is God's Word, we take what it says literally. Sometimes God speaks to us directly; sometimes he uses figures or symbols. To allow God to speak for himself, then, is to let the Bible tell us when it is speaking directly and when it is speaking in word pictures. Many of the false interpretations of Revelation come from breaking this rule. To avoid this mistake, we must look carefully at the words that lead up to passages we have questions about. The words themselves will tell us when John is speaking directly and when he is describing the visions the Spirit gave to him. We will blur Revelation's message if we take John's direct words as figurative or assign literalistic meaning to his picture language.

We approach the picture language of Revelation in the same way we study symbolic language in other parts of Scripture. First, we remember that John's visions are like large, beautiful paintings. Like Jesus' parables, each picture has one point of focus that conveys a single lesson. Individual details contribute to the overall beauty of a vision but must not detract our attention from the main point. So, much the same as we would do in one of Jesus' parables, in John's visions we will look for the main point of John's visions, without forcing some meaning from every detail.

Scripture provides its own explanation for Revelation's vivid images. The Bible's clear passages help us understand those that are less clear to us. For instance, John explains many of his own word pictures, just as Jesus frequently did in his parables. Sometimes, when John does not immediately explain his symbols, he will clarify them later in the book. Some pictures that are not explained within the Revelation become clear when we compare them to similar pictures in other parts of the Bible. The meaning of a few of John's pictures will remain hidden to us.

Along with our confidence that the Bible is God's Word is our trust that God provides all that is necessary for our faith and knowledge. So, even though we may not understand all of John's figurative language, we will not force any meaning on his words that Scripture does not support.

If we let God speak for himself, his words also will influence the way we follow from one vision to another in the Revelation. The way Jesus speaks through John prevents us from reading the seven visions like chapters in a novel. John often notes the passing of time by saying "after this" or "then." But he is usually marking time that passed for him since his last vision. Only the content of the visions themselves can tell us if time passes from one vision to the next. So we notice that several visions will picture the same time in history, only from different angles.

The Revelation describes the end times before Jesus' return—the times we are living in now. John's seven visions go back and forth over the ongoing struggle between Christ and Satan. God's army includes Jesus, the holy angels, saints, and faithful witnesses to the gospel. The devil's forces include Satan, his evil angels, unbelievers, false prophets, and worldly government. While all the visions describe the same battle, each pictures different combatants and arenas of conflict. Each successive vision shows the battle growing more intense. The last vision climaxes with Jesus' final defeat of Satan and his eternal victory for the saints.

God wisely arranged that Revelation be placed at the end of the Bible. A good background in all the Scriptures will provide readers of Revelation a double blessing. It will keep us from putting our own ideas into this book and help us receive more of God's rich comfort from it.

The meaning of the numbers in Revelation

Numbers are part of Jesus' picture language in the Revelation. Although not every number in this book is symbolical, Jesus often uses numbers not to give us a factual count, but to represent certain spiritual truths. To learn the meaning of numbers, we first look at how Jesus uses them, then how the rest of Scripture employs them. We must not read anything into figurative numbers that contradicts what the Bible says in literal terms. Yet, when numbers recall Bible truths, they enrich our understanding of the visions. The chart below shows the symbolic use of numbers within Revelation. The commentary will note when numbers correlate to other parts of the Bible.

3 The number of God: the three Persons of the holy Trinity at the throne (1:4,5): threefold, three-verse praise of the living creatures (4:8); salvation, power, and kingdom of God (12:10); 30 references to "the Lamb" (14:1 and others); salvation, glory, and power (19:1).

4 The number of the created world, the earth, and all people: "the four living creatures" (4:8), representing the created world; four horsemen riding the earth (6:1-8); nation, tribe, people and language (7:9; 11:9), representing all people; four angels, four corners of the earth, and four winds of the earth (7:1); four-sided Holy City and four gates (21:13).

6 The number of evil, deception, and things that are imperfect or incomplete: the number of the beast is 666 (13:18).

7 The sum of God's number (3) and man's number (4) equals God's gracious interaction with the world: the seven spirits before the throne (1:4; 4:5; 5:6); the seven lampstands, stars, and churches (2,3); God's covenant of grace, the seven visions of Revelation; the scroll with the seven seals (5:1); sevenfold praise of the elders

and living creatures (5:12); sevenfold praise of the angels (7:12); the seven trumpets (8:6); half of seven, $3^1/_2$: 42 months is $3^1/_2$ years (11:2); 1,260 days is $3^1/_2$ years (11:3; 12:6); $3^1/_2$ days is half a week (11:9,11).

10 The number of completion, an amount designated and limited by God: "ten days" of persecution for the members of the congregation at Smyrna (2:10); ten thousand times ten thousand angels (5:11); half of ten, five (9:5,10); ten horns (12:3; 13:1; 17:12); ten times ten times ten, a thousand (20:2-7).

12 The product of God's number (3) and man's number (4); thus, the result of God's gracious work among men, that is, the church: 24 elders (4:4; 19:4); 12 tribes of Israel (7:4-8; 21:12); 144,000 elect (7:4; 14:1,3); 12 apostles (21:14); the measurements of the Holy City (21:12-21); the tree of life (22:2).

Theme and Outline

JESUS ASSURES OUR VICTORY!

I. INTRODUCTION 1:1-11
   A. Revelation from Jesus to John 1:1,2
   B. Blessings and greetings 1:3-5
   C. Praise for the Savior 1:5-8
   D. The occasion for writing 1:9-11

II. VISION OF THE SEVEN LETTERS 1:12–3:22
   A. Jesus wrote the letters 1:12-20
   B. The first letter: to Ephesus 2:1-7
   C. The second letter: to Smyrna 2:8-11
   D. The third letter: to Pergamum 2:12-17

INTRODUCTION
(1:1-11)

Revelation from Jesus to John

1 **The revelation of Jesus Christ, which God gave him to show his servants what must soon take place. He made it known by sending his angel to his servant John, ²who testifies to everything he saw—that is, the word of God and the testimony of Jesus Christ.**

With these simple words John introduces a most profound letter. "The revelation" (verse 1) is English for the Greek word *apocalypse*. It means the unveiling of something that previously was hidden. In Revelation Jesus will unfold as much as we need to know in order to face the future. He wants us to be fully confident of his final victory over our enemies. What God is about to reveal is for the sake of his servants, his people, his church. Revelation speaks to God's servants in every age. What Jesus gave John to write is for our benefit.

Skeptics, of course, deny the inspired quality and prophetic nature of John's Revelation. They say that John wrote only about what already had taken place or what was happening as he wrote. But John dispels these doubts. He credits Jesus as the real author. In this book, John says, Jesus will reveal through him "what must soon take place" (verse 1). What Jesus gives him to write is a divine revelation of the future. The prophecies in this book "must" take place because the God who knows the future controls the future.

The way John weaves "the revelation of Jesus Christ" in verse 1 together with "the word of God and the testimony of

Jesus Christ" in verse 2 emphasizes that these are not John's private thoughts. He is testifying as a witness to what he saw. Instead of saying he heard it, John writes that he "saw" the Word of God (verse 2). He talks this way because Jesus communicated the contents of this book through a series of visions. John "saw" the message in the same way Old Testament prophets, or seers, did—that is, by means of visions (1:11). Through these visions Jesus drew away the curtain of time to reveal to John's eyes the great drama yet to unfold for his church.

God first gave this revelation to Jesus. All that Jesus tells us came from the Father (John 14:10; Hebrews 1:1,2). What Jesus received from the Father he then gave to his angel to relay, in turn, to John. John carefully traces the source of his message so his readers can be confident that what he writes, like the rest of inspired Scriptures, is "God-breathed" (2 Timothy 3:16).

Blessings and greetings

³Blessed is the one who reads the words of this prophecy, and blessed are those who hear it and take to heart what is written in it, because the time is near.

⁴John,

To the seven churches in the province of Asia:

Grace and peace to you from him who is, and who was, and who is to come, and from the seven spirits before his throne, ⁵and from Jesus Christ, who is the faithful witness, the first-born from the dead, and the ruler of the kings of the earth.

The lector, that is, the one who reads this book of prophecy in public worship, will be blessed. To be blessed means to be among those whom God makes spiritually happy. John promises this same inner peace to the members of the congregation who hear it, read it, and take it to heart. John is restating the Savior's promise in Luke 11:28: "Blessed . . . are those who hear the word of God and obey it." The promise of blessing invites a conscious listening, and through this God produces faith and willing obedience.

The things that are about to take place will happen "soon" (verse 1). The prophecies of Revelation have unfolded quickly for everyone who has ever read them. Each of us is born into the middle of the great strife between Christ and Satan. It is a short "seventy years" (Psalm 90:10) from the time we are born until we share in the great victory Jesus promises each of his servants.

First, John introduced Jesus as the real author. Then he stated the purpose for writing: to strengthen Jesus' servants for the battle to come. Now John follows the customary form of greeting for letters of that time. He introduces himself as the actual writer and then addresses the seven congregations in the province of Asia as his readers. At that time Asia Minor was a province of the Roman Empire. Today it is eastern Turkey (see map on page vi).

When John addressed the churches, he was not speaking about worship buildings or formally organized congregations. None of the early Christian churches had public buildings for worship as we know them today. Most met in homes; a few may have met in synagogues. By the word *churches*, then, John is referring to the readers as people who belong to God. To those gathered around the Word and sacraments at these seven localities, Jesus will now give the reassurance of his final victory.

John greets his readers with the same "grace and peace" that Paul (1 Thessalonians 1:1) and Peter (1 Peter 1:2) used to open their letters. Grace is the undeserved pardon that God gave us in Jesus. It is a one-sided, forgiving love. Peace is the Greek equivalent of the Hebrew word *shalom*. God's forgiving love in the heart of the believer produces this peace. It comes from knowing that Jesus satisfied God's anger over our sins and has declared an end to the war between himself and the sinner. It is the quiet confidence that God is on our side in life's daily struggle.

Grace and peace come from the triune God. John mentions each person of God. He "who is, and who was, and who is to come" is the Father. John's choice of words reflects the changeless nature of Jehovah expressed in Exodus 3:14: "I AM WHO I AM." God does not change. He keeps his promises. Even "if we are faithless, he will remain faithful, for he cannot disown himself" (2 Timothy 2:13). The Father is committed to our salvation; he is unchanged by our lapses into sin and forgives us for the sake of his Son's peace-making work.

John depicts the third person of God as "the seven spirits before [God's] throne" (verse 4). John may have chosen these words to reflect the seven descriptions of the Spirit in Isaiah 11:2. If he did, his words could be translated "the seven-fold Spirit." There is no doubt, however, that John is speaking about the Holy Spirit. In 3:1, 4:5, and 5:6, John says the seven spirits are "of God." In 1:4 the seven spirits are positioned between the Father and Jesus Christ. Jesus promised that the Father would send the Spirit in his name (John 14:26). These are "the seven spirits of God sent out into all the earth" (5:6) with the message of Jesus Christ.

John mentions the second person of the Trinity by name: "Jesus Christ" (verse 5). While speaking to the Pharisees, Jesus made the claim that God was his authority. He said, "He who sent me is reliable, and what I have heard from him I tell the world" (John 8:26). Jesus spoke only what the Father gave him to say. This makes him "the faithful witness" (verse 5). Jesus' faithful testimony also makes him the great Prophet that Moses promised God would send (Deuteronomy 18:15; see also Jeremiah 23:28; Hebrews 1:1,2).

On Easter morning Jesus became "the firstborn from the dead" (verse 5). The firstborn in Jewish families was the pacesetter. Other sons and daughters were blessed in line with the inheritance the firstborn received. By his death and resurrection, our High Priest, Jesus, became the pacesetter among the children of God. Through him we have salvation and regular access to God's throne. "Because Jesus lives forever, he has a permanent priesthood. Therefore he is able to save completely those who come to God through him, because he always lives to intercede for them" (Hebrews 7:24,25). When we die, we inherit an eternal benefit from his resurrection. Jesus promised, "Because I live, you also will live" (John 14:19). All who are God's children by faith will be blessed in line with the resurrection of the firstborn from the dead. "The Lord Jesus Christ . . . by the power that enables him to bring everything under his control, will transform our lowly bodies so that they will be like his glorious body" (Philippians 3:20,21).

The great Prophet, the great Priest is also our great King. All power has been given to Jesus in heaven and on earth. In times of deepest distress, believers know that he is in control, not just of spiritual things, but also of the affairs of this world. Jesus is "King of kings and Lord of lords" (19:16). History is his story; earthly rulers are temporary pretenders to the real throne (Psalm 2). "At the name of Jesus every knee should bow" (Philippians 2:10).

Throughout verses 4 and 5 John uses some unusual Greek grammar for the descriptive names of God. The fact that he uses these unusual forms for all three persons of God indicates that the three persons are one in essence. The forms themselves stress the unchangeable nature of all three persons. As the Father was faithful in sending his Son, so the Spirit is faithful in dispensing his gifts, and the Son in governing history for the good of his people.

Praise for the Savior

To him who loves us and has freed us from our sins by his blood, ⁶and has made us to be a kingdom and priests to serve his God and Father—to him be glory and power for ever and ever! Amen.

⁷ **Look, he is coming with the clouds,**
and every eye will see him,
even those who pierced him;
and all the peoples of the earth will mourn
because of him.

So shall it be! Amen.

⁸**"I am the Alpha and the Omega," says the Lord God, "who is, and who was, and who is to come, the Almighty."**

Now we see why John listed the persons of the Trinity as Father, Spirit, and Son. He continues with a song of tribute to the last-mentioned Jesus. This doxology is directed to "him who loves us" (verse 5). The Greek language has three different words for love. John chose the one he used in John 3:16 to depict the Father's undeserved love for the world. Jesus' ongoing affection for us moved him to break the chains of our sin's guilt, punishment, and power.

In the Old Testament, God promised his covenant people, "You will be for me a kingdom of priests and a holy nation" (Exodus 19:6). Jesus also makes us, the ones he loves and forgives, to be "a kingdom and priests" (verse 6). As members of his kingdom, we began our reign at the moment we were brought to faith. Paul writes, "God raised us up with Christ and seated us with him in the heavenly realms in

Christ Jesus" (Ephesians 2:6). In this kingdom "all things are yours" (1 Corinthians 3:21). Every joy and privilege of kingdom membership begins now and continues throughout the New Testament age.

Jesus made us members of his kingdom for a purpose: "to serve his God and Father" (verse 6). Our service is to offer up sacrifices as his priests. Our great Priest, Jesus, completed the perfect sacrifice for our sins. "By one sacrifice he has made perfect forever those who are being made holy" (Hebrews 10:14). Since our sins were taken away by his sacrifice, "there is no longer any sacrifice for sin" (Hebrews 10:18). Still, John says, we are priests for Christ. We are "a holy priesthood, offering spiritual sacrifices acceptable to God through Jesus Christ" (1 Peter 2:5). But the sacrifices Jesus' priests bring to God are not offerings to pay for sin; they are thank-offerings. Thankfully we "declare the praises of him who called [us] out of darkness into his wonderful light" (1 Peter 2:9). We offer our "bodies as living sacrifices, holy and pleasing to God—this is [our] spiritual act of worship" (Romans 12:1). In Jesus' kingdom the priesthood means the daily life Christians live to please God.

Those who rule with Christ in his kingdom and serve as his priests give all the credit—all "glory and power" (verse 6)—to Jesus. With a loud amen we all rejoice that this is most certainly true of us. Right now, our privileges in the kingdom are not apparent to the world around us. "For you died, and your life is now hidden with Christ in God" (Colossians 3:4). But that will change soon. "When Christ, who is your life, appears, then you also will appear with him in glory" (Colossians 3:4). The reign that begins now with Jesus continues into eternity. Members of his kingdom "will reign for ever and ever" (22:5). The lives of happy service we began on earth will continue in perfect bliss in heaven: "His servants will serve him. They will seek his face, and his name will be on their foreheads" (22:3,4).

To reestablish the victory theme of his letter, John launches into a hymn of praise to this Jesus who has made us kings and priests. More than two dozen times in this book John will call us to attention with the word "Look!" Here he recalls the promise of the angels at Jesus' ascension: "This same Jesus, who has been taken from you into heaven, will come back in the same way you have seen him go into heaven" (Acts 1:11). He will come back as he left, "with the clouds" (verse 7).

Scripture holds up the pierced hands and feet of the Savior as a sign of his humble but victorious struggle for our salvation. David prophesied, "They have pierced my hands and my feet" (Psalm 22:16). Isaiah said God's suffering servant would be "pierced for our transgressions" (53:5). Zechariah echoes, "They will look on me, the one they have pierced" (12:10). This trail of prophecy will end when the enemies who pierced Jesus by sin or sword stand before his judgment. "Every eye will see him" (verse 7) because all will be raised from the dead (Daniel 12:2). The majority will be those who rejected their Lord through unbelief and opposed his church. "Broad is the road that leads to destruction, and many enter through it" (Matthew 7:13). "There will be weeping and gnashing of teeth" (Matthew 22:13) because it is too late to repent. But for the faithful, Jesus' promise will come true: "I will see you again and you will rejoice" (John 16:22). "He will wipe every tear from their eyes" (Revelation 21:4).

The one who will do the final judging on the Last Day identifies himself as "the Alpha and the Omega" (verse 8). Even though John says "the Lord God" said these words, we know that it is the Son, not the Father speaking. Jesus will identify himself with this same name two more times (21:6; 22:13). In 22:13 he explains the name: "I am the Alpha and the Omega, the First and the Last, the Beginning and the End." A little later in this chapter Jesus calls himself "the First and the Last" (1:17).

Alpha and Omega are the first and last letters of the Greek alphabet. Jesus uses these letters for his name to symbolize God's steadfastness from beginning to end. He brought us to faith and will stay with us to the end. We can be confident "that he who began a good work in [us] will carry it on to completion" (Philippians 1:6). Jesus is "the author and perfecter of our faith" (Hebrews 12:2). Words used to describe the Father—who is and who was and who is to come (1:4)— also fit the Son: "Jesus Christ is the same yesterday and today and forever" (Hebrews 13:8).

The occasion for writing

⁹**I, John, your brother and companion in the suffering and kingdom and patient endurance that are ours in Jesus, was on the island of Patmos because of the word of God and the testimony of Jesus. ¹⁰On the Lord's Day I was in the Spirit, and I heard behind me a loud voice like a trumpet, ¹¹which said: "Write on a scroll what you see and send it to the seven churches: to Ephesus, Smyrna, Pergamum, Thyatira, Sardis, Philadelphia and Laodicea."**

In verse 9 John introduces himself again, this time to put himself on the same level as his readers. He is their brother. No doubt he counts it a privilege to be numbered with them. "The suffering and kingdom and patient endurance" (verse 9) belong to all believers. We share them. They belong to us because we are "in Jesus" (verse 9), that is, we are connected to him by faith. Peter encouraged his readers, "Rejoice that you participate in the sufferings of Christ, so that you may be overjoyed when his glory is revealed" (1 Peter 4:13). Paul wrote, "We also rejoice in our sufferings" (Romans 5:3).

Like the other apostles, John views suffering for Jesus as a reason to rejoice. His readers also needed to see their troubles from this perspective. Many of the Christians in Asia Minor were suffering because of their faith in Jesus. Some were openly persecuted. As he writes from exile, John is their brother both in faith and in suffering for the faith. He is not talking down to them; he is speaking as one of them, their "companion" (verse 9).

John was exiled to Patmos, a desolate island in the Aegean Sea. Less than 50 square miles in size, it lies off the Asia Minor mainland, southwest of the city of Ephesus. For his preaching and teaching about Jesus, the Romans banished John there as an enemy of the state. We do not have the details of John's exile, neither the exact circumstances nor the duration of it. But we know that the apostle can address suffering Christians with empathy and not mere sympathy. A companion is literally someone who shares something with others. John shared with his readers their suffering for the sake of the Word of God.

John received his vision from Jesus "on the Lord's Day" (verse 10), that is, on the day the Lord rose from the dead— Sunday. Although the phrase occurs only here in the New Testament, the fact that John uses it without explanation means that his readers were used to speaking of their day of worship this way (compare 1 Corinthians 16:2). By choosing to worship on Sunday, the early Christians expressed the freedom that the Lord's resurrection gave them from the Old Testament ceremonial observance of the seventh day, Saturday.

The NIV translation says John was "in the Spirit" (verse 10). But John wrote simply that he was "in spirit," that is, in a certain spiritual mood. Referring to this same state of mind,

John speaks of being "in spirit" again in 4:2, 17:3, and 21:10. When John mentions the Holy Spirit in Revelation, he pictures him as "the seven spirits" (1:4; 3:1; 4:5; 5:6) or calls him "*the* Spirit" (2:7,11,17,29; 3:6,13,22; 22:17). John was in a spiritual mood, deep in thought with Bible study and prayer. God led him to a state of mind that was receptive to what Jesus was about to reveal to him.

While John was in this frame of mind, "a loud voice" came to him (verse 10). It was like a trumpet, that is, loud and clear. There is no indication that John was seeking or expecting a revelation. This was God's doing. The voice came from behind him. John was only a scribe for the inspired revelation. Jesus provided the message and designated the intended audience. John was to send what he wrote on a scroll to the seven churches of Asia Minor (see map on page vi).

VISION OF THE SEVEN LETTERS
(1:12–3:22)

Jesus wrote the letters

¹²I turned around to see the voice that was speaking to me. And when I turned I saw seven golden lampstands, ¹³and among the lampstands was someone "like a son of man," dressed in a robe reaching down to his feet and with a golden sash around his chest. ¹⁴His head and hair were white like wool, as white as snow, and his eyes were like blazing fire. ¹⁵His feet were like bronze glowing in a furnace, and his voice was like the sound of rushing waters. ¹⁶In his right hand he held seven stars, and out of his mouth came a sharp double-edged sword. His face was like the sun shining in all its brilliance.

¹⁷When I saw him, I fell at his feet as though dead. Then he placed his right hand on me and said: "Do not be afraid. I am the First and the Last. ¹⁸I am the Living One; I was dead, and behold I am alive for ever and ever! And I hold the keys of death and Hades.

¹⁹Write, therefore, what you have seen, what is now and what will take place later. ²⁰The mystery of the seven stars that you saw in my right hand and of the seven golden lampstands is this: The seven stars are the angels of the seven churches, and the seven lampstands are the seven churches."

John's reaction was natural. He turned to "see" the voice (verse 12). He wanted to see who belonged to the voice that was talking to him. But at first he did not see to whom the voice belonged. Instead, when he turned around, he saw seven lampstands. The unnatural phenomena of the voice and the lampstands begin the first of seven visions John will relate in Revelation.

Later, John explains that the lampstands he saw represent the seven churches to whom the letter is addressed (verse 20). Among the lampstands John noticed "someone 'like a son of man'" (verse 13). Bible writers like Ezekiel used "son of man" in a general way to refer to a human figure. Although Jesus often called himself *the* Son of Man, New Testament writers on their own never call him that. It is clear that the human figure John sees is Jesus. Yet, since John says "a" son of man, he is speaking here in a general way of seeing someone in human form, as he does again in chapter 14, verse 14. Jesus' presence among the lampstands illustrates the promise he gave to his church: "Surely I am with you always, to the very end of the age" (Matthew 28:20; see also Matthew 18:20).

The description of this human form confirms that this is the same Jesus who called himself the Son of Man. First, the vision pictures the great High Priest serving his people. Jesus is surrounded by details reminiscent of the Old Testament priests, not only the lampstands (verse 12; Exodus 25:31-40), but also the long priestly robe tied with a golden sash (verse 13; Exodus 28:4,8). In his vision seven hundred years earlier, Isaiah saw "the Lord seated on a throne, high and exalted, and the train of his robe filled the temple" (Isaiah 6:1). The robe John mentions signifies the same dignity and authority. The white hair stands for God's holiness and agelessness. Daniel uses similar word pictures in his vision: "The Ancient of Days took his seat. His clothing was as white as snow; the hair of his head was white like wool" (Daniel 7:9).

The blazing eyes call to mind the scrutiny and wisdom of a great ruler who cares for his subjects and opposes their enemies. "The eyes of the LORD are on the righteous and his ears are attentive to their cry; the face of the LORD is against those who do evil" (Psalm 34:15,16). This is the great King from whom nothing is hidden. "Nothing in all creation is hidden from God's sight. Everything is uncovered and laid bare before the eyes of him to whom we must give account" (Hebrews 4:13). The bronze feet will make his enemies his footstool: "For he must reign until he has put all his enemies under his feet" (1 Corinthians 15:25). When the King lifts his thundering voice (Ezekiel 43:2), "the earth melts" (Psalm 46:6). King Jesus rules on behalf of his church. "God placed all things under his feet and appointed him to be head over everything for the church" (Ephesians 1:22). In John's vision the church is represented by the seven lampstands. Jesus is always present among the lampstands as he is always present among his faithful people.

The great Prophet holds the seven stars in his right hand (verse 16). Verse 20 explains that the seven stars are the messengers in the churches who proclaim the Word of God. These preachers carry the double-edged sword of the great Prophet, Jesus. This sword is the twofold message of law and gospel: "Whoever believes in the Son has eternal life, but whoever rejects the Son will not see life, for God's wrath remains on him" (John 3:36). It is "the sword of the Spirit, which is the word of God" (Ephesians 6:17); the Word of God is "living and active" and "sharper than any two-edged sword" (Hebrews 4:12).

The appearance of his face reasserts the divine nature of this human figure. John saw this face before, at the Transfiguration. There Jesus gave his disciples a preview of his divine glory. Matthew wrote, "His face shone like the sun" (Matthew 17:2). This is the same Jesus, now ascended to the glory of God in heaven.

John fainted from fear of standing in the presence of God (verse 17). Jesus comforted him with words that apply to every sinner who fears the blinding light of God's holy presence: "Do not be afraid" (verse 17). Jesus also gives us the reason why we don't have to fear the face of God: "I am the First and the Last" (verse 18). Jesus is the same Alpha and Omega of verse 8. By his very nature he is the eternal God. He became fully human so that his physical resurrection can guarantee safety from death to everyone who believes in him. "Because I live, you also will live" (John 14:19), he promised. The God-man, our Prophet, Priest, and King, holds the keys (Matthew 16:18,19) that lock the door to eternal death in hell (see 20:1).

Now that John knows who belongs to the voice, Jesus repeats his command (verse 11) for John to write. Then, in two different ways, he describes the content of the inspired message to follow. We must note both of these descriptions to interpret properly what John is about to write. John was to write "what you have seen" and "what is now and what will take place later" (verse 19).

In Revelation John wrote what he saw. He saw visions, a series of detailed paintings, full of eye-catching detail. Keep in mind that the real author of Revelation, the one who reveals these images, is Jesus. He stands at the center of the visions John saw. Jesus and his message to churches then and now is the focus of these visions. The bright details attract us to Jesus without detracting our attention from his message.

As John wrote about what he saw, he was also writing about "what is now and what will take place later" (verse 19). The seven visions of Revelation will demonstrate how history repeats itself in the future of Christ's church. The visions are the story of "what is" at John's time and a revelation of "what will take place later." Each vision is one in a series of snapshots taken from different angles. These varying pictures give us a composite view of one ongoing struggle that leads through strife to final victory. Through John's visions we view the same battle being fought on different fronts at the same time: on earth, in heaven, and in hell. Through these visions all believers on all fields of battle and at every stage of the fight gain the confidence of final victory. The Jesus who stands in the center of all the visions will win the victory for them.

Many of Revelation's symbols are explained for us. Verse 20 gives us an example of Revelation explaining what a symbol means. Jesus tells us that the seven stars are the seven angels of the seven churches. An angel is a messenger. In the Bible these messengers are most often heavenly ones, such as the angel Gabriel. Here, however, the angels are the human messengers that bring Jesus' message to his churches. They are the pastors and teachers and missionaries in our churches today. The seven lampstands are the seven churches among whom the great High Priest walks. When John announced the birth of Jesus in his Gospel, he wrote, "The true light that gives light to every man was coming into the world" (John 1:9). Jesus asks us in turn to share the light he brings to his church: "In the same way, let your light shine before men" (Matthew 5:16).

The first letter: to Ephesus

2 "To the angel of the church in Ephesus write:

These are the words of him who holds the seven stars in his right hand and walks among the seven golden lampstands: ²I know your deeds, your hard work and your perseverance. I know that you cannot tolerate wicked men, that you have tested those who claim to be apostles but are not, and have found them false. ³You have persevered and have endured hardships for my name, and have not grown weary.

⁴**Yet I hold this against you: You have forsaken your first love.** ⁵**Remember the height from which you have fallen! Repent and do the things you did at first. If you do not repent, I will come to you and remove your lampstand from its place.** ⁶**But you have this in your favor: You hate the practices of the Nicolaitans, which I also hate.**

⁷**He who has an ear, let him hear what the Spirit says to the churches. To him who overcomes, I will give the right to eat from the tree of life, which is in the paradise of God.**

As Jesus begins his personal message to individual churches in Asia Minor, he addresses them in the same order he mentioned them in 1:11. The order seems to be geographical (see map on page vi). He begins with Ephesus and proceeds clockwise around the region. The seven churches of Asia Minor are real congregations addressed at this time in history. There is no indication that these seven churches should be understood symbolically. Jesus' message to them, however, is timeless. The warnings and comfort he offers apply to the church in every age.

It is striking how Jesus addresses the churches with the *singular* "you" (verse 2) in this and in the other six letters. He is speaking to the pastor as the representative of all the people under his care. Yet it is clear that the whole congregation is meant by "you," because our Lord briefly uses the plural "you" in chapter 2, verses 10 and 23 to 25. The effect is that each hearer would receive Jesus' words as directed specifically to him or her.

Right after the address to the angel (verse 1) John identifies the speaker. Yes, John wrote the words down, and someone else would deliver the letter to each of the pastors. But Jesus introduces himself as the one speaking to each church. The pastor, or messenger, would be glad to hear that Jesus holds the seven stars, that is, the seven angels (1:20), in his right hand. The Savior's right hand is the strength he exerts to protect his people. Pastors trust that Jesus is holding them in his right hand as they guide their churches through the troubled last days. The Savior who upholds the spiritual leaders of our churches is present at all times with the members too. As he walks among the seven lampstands, his churches, he keeps his promise "Where two or three come together in my name, there am I with them" (Matthew 18:20).

"Lord, you know all things" (John 21:17), Peter confessed. The omniscient "eyes . . . like blazing fire" (1:14) knew the deeds of the Ephesians too (verse 2). First, Jesus commends them for what he saw. The Ephesians were a hardworking congregation. They were founded and pastored by faithful, hardworking ministers. Paul had labored as a missionary for three years in Ephesus (Acts 20:31). Later, Timothy (1 Timothy 1:3) and Apollos (Acts 18:24-26) served there. Early church tradition holds that John came there about ten years after Paul left, in the late 60s, A.D. The hardworking Ephesians prove the observation that congregations often take on the character of the pastors who serve them.

Twice, in verses 2 and 3, Jesus commends them for their perseverance. They patiently bore up under hardships. Also, sandwiched between two commendations for patience, Jesus praises them for their intolerance of wicked men and false apostles. We often hear that we are unloving when we refuse to work with churches that don't accept all the Bible's teachings. But here Jesus teaches that resistance to moral evil and false teaching is entirely consistent with Christian patience. The Ephesians were "speaking the truth in love" (Ephesians 4:15) when they tested the claims of the false apostles against the teachings they received from Paul, Apollos, and Timothy. It is false ecumenism when churches work together without first agreeing on what the work of the church is.

"Wicked men" (verse 2) means those who are morally evil. They are lowlifes. False apostles attempted to lead the Ephesians astray with fake teaching credentials. Some years before, Paul predicted the Ephesians would encounter such false teachers. He warned their elders, "Savage wolves will come in among you and will not spare the flock" (Acts 20:29). When Jesus says they "have not grown weary" (verse 3), he means they endured hardships for a long time and were still holding firm at the time he wrote.

Jesus' letter to the Ephesians forms a general pattern he will use in all seven letters to the churches. First, he commands John to write; then he identifies himself and commends and/or scolds the congregation; finally, he closes with a promise joined with a plea to listen to what the Spirit is saying to them.

Now Jesus must point to a problem: the Ephesians had lost their first love (verse 4). Only the blazing eyes of the omniscient Savior can see what is missing from the heart. Years earlier, Paul wrote of the Ephesians' "love for all the saints" (Ephesians 1:15) and prayed that they would continue to be "rooted and established in love" (3:17). But now, as their love for their Savior grew cold, they began to act in a loveless way toward one another. They were still working hard, but their activity stemmed more from a sense of duty than love.

At one time the Ephesians knew "how wide and long and high and deep is the love of Christ" (Ephesians 3:18). But as their appreciation of Christ's love eroded, they fell from this height. There was only one way back. Jesus urged them along this road to the lofty love they once knew: "Repent!" (verse 5). *Repent* literally means "have a change of mind." Repentance is a double change that turns the heart away from one thing and toward another. Jesus' call to turn away from sin and back to his love is itself the power that makes repentance happen.

The invisible repentance that God works in the heart never remains hidden there. It displays itself in an outward change of life. So Jesus urges, "Do the things you did at first" (verse 5). John the Baptist also demanded that those who repented demonstrate their change of heart: "Produce fruit in keeping with repentance" (Matthew 3:8). Renewed in the Savior's love, the Ephesians would again display their first "love for all the saints" (Ephesians 1:15).

With his call to repent, Jesus issued a loving warning about the consequences of not heeding his call. He would come and remove their lampstand (verse 5). From our Lord's words, we can see that the lampstand is the symbol of God's grace among his people. The threat to remove the lampstand warns us that when a congregation despises the gospel, God will eventually remove his means of grace from them. Today the once proud city of Ephesus no longer exists. No Christian congregation gathers there around the gospel in Word and sacraments. The lampstand is gone. The Savior's loving warning to Ephesus is also his call to every modern congregation.

In verse 6, Jesus adds a final word of commendation. He tells the Ephesians that their hate for the practices of the Nicolaitans was in their favor. The "practices" of the Nicolaitans are mentioned here and their false "teaching" in verse 15. We know very little about the Nicolaitans, except that they troubled the churches both in Ephesus and Pergamum. From the brief mention of the Nicolaitans by early church writers, some suggest that this group encouraged open immorality. They may have taught that since we are fully forgiven, we can live any way we want to. This wrong-headed thinking denies that the fruit of repentance is willing obedi-

ence. But we need to know no more. The point is that hating
false teachings and practices is consistent with loving Jesus.

The letter closes with an appeal to listen: "He who has an
ear, let him hear what the Spirit says to the churches" (verse
7). The Creator gave us ears, and the Holy Spirit inspired
these words of correction and comfort. Thus God has provided everything his churches need for spiritual renewal.
Those who fail to respond can blame only themselves. This
appeal echoes those Jesus offered during his earthly ministry:
"He who has ears, let him hear" (Matthew 11:15; see also
Matthew 13:9,43; Mark 4:23).

Jesus attached a promise to his appeal to listen. This
promise demonstrates that his appeal is also an invitation of
grace. Jesus wants all to be part of the victory celebration
around "the tree of life, which is in the paradise of God"
(verse 7). The word *paradise*, or "garden park," calls to mind
the garden of Eden, where God first put the tree of life (Genesis 2:9). Because of sin, man never ate of that tree. God
barred him from it so he would not live forever in his sinful
condition (Genesis 3:22-24). But here the promise "to him
who overcomes" (verse 7)—a similar phrase occurs at the
end of each of the seven letters—looks to the future when
they will "have the right to the tree of life" in heaven (22:14).

The second letter: to Smyrna

⁸"To the angel of the church in Smyrna write:

These are the words of him who is the First and the
Last, who died and came to life again. ⁹I know your afflictions and your poverty—yet you are rich! I know the slander of those who say they are Jews and are not, but are a
synagogue of Satan. ¹⁰Do not be afraid of what you are
about to suffer. I tell you, the devil will put some of you in
prison to test you, and you will suffer persecution for ten

**days. Be faithful, even to the point of death, and I will
give you the crown of life.**

**¹¹He who has an ear, let him hear what the Spirit says
to the churches. He who overcomes will not be hurt at all
by the second death.**

Only two of the seven congregations receive commendation without criticism. Smyrna is one of them. Jesus directs John to write his letter to the angel of this church. The angel of the church is its messenger, its head elder. Today we would call him the pastor of the congregation.

Jesus introduces himself to Smyrna with some of the same words he used to reveal himself to John at the beginning of the vision (1:17,18). Jesus is "the First and the Last" (verse 8). As true God, he is eternal and unchangeable, "the same yesterday and today and forever" (Hebrews 13:8). He is also true man, "who died and came to life again" (verse 8). What they are about to hear "are the words of him" (verse 8), the eternal God who entered history to be their Savior. "He was delivered over to death for our sins and was raised to life for our justification" (Romans 4:25).

In the middle of trouble, we often wonder whether God knows or cares about our situation. Twice in verse 9 Jesus says he knows. The fact that he mentions it also shows that he cares. He knows all about the afflictions and poverty at Smyrna. We cannot be sure of what caused their problems. The Romans may have imprisoned them and confiscated their property for refusing to worship the emperor, or the congregation may have suffered religious persecution and economic discrimination from their townsmen.

No matter what made them poor, the Lord who knows and cares interjects, "Yet you are rich!" (verse 9). Smyrna is the opposite of the materially rich but spiritually poor Laodicean church (3:17,18). The poverty Smyrna incurred by its faithfulness to Jesus had stored up for them "treasures in heaven" (Matthew 6:20). This congregation typifies believers everywhere: "poor, yet making many rich; having nothing, and yet possessing everything" (2 Corinthians 6:10).

"The slander of those who say they are Jews and are not" (verse 9) added to Smyrna's troubles. Ever since Paul began his missionary work among them, Jews throughout Asia Minor had slandered Christians. They told Christians they were not God's children unless they were physically descended from Abraham or conformed to Moses' circumcision. But Jesus had taught Jews during his earthly ministry that the real descendants of Abraham were those who "hold to [his] teaching" (John 8:31). And Paul assured the Romans, "A man is a Jew if he is one inwardly; and circumcision is circumcision of the heart, by the Spirit, not by the written code. Such a man's praise is not from men, but from God" (Romans 2:29).

In the face of slander by evil men, the believers at Smyrna were content to live with God's praise. Jesus knew their faithfulness. His all-seeing eyes knew that the slanderers were really a "synagogue of Satan" (verse 9). During his earthly ministry, Jesus told Jews who claimed to be children of God because of their physical heritage, "You belong to your father, the devil" (John 8:44). In the same way, he speaks of the Jews who slandered the believers at Smyrna. Although they "say they are Jews," they "are not" (verse 9).

The devil was the source of other problems this congregation had to face. Before our Lord states the details, he comforts them: "Do not be afraid of what you are about to suffer" (verse 10). To the 12 disciples on storm-tossed waters and to the three disciples facedown from fright on the Mount of Transfiguration, Jesus offered the same comfort: "Don't be afraid" (Matthew 14:27; 17:7).

"The devil will put some of you in prison to test you, and you will suffer persecution for ten days" (verse 10). It is possible that "ten days" is meant literally. But in John's visions numbers are frequently used to represent something symbolically. "Ten days" may represent a limited time, as in Genesis 24:55, or a specific amount of time, fixed by God. Regardless of how we read "ten days," it means that God knows what troubles his people face and limits the influence of evil on his children.

No matter who the human agents are, the devil is always behind the persecution that tests believers. "Our struggle is not against flesh and blood, but . . . against the spiritual forces of evil" (Ephesians 6:12). "Satan" (verse 9), who led the Jews to slander, is the proper name for the devil mentioned in verse 10. The devil and Satan are said to be the same in chapter 20, where we learn that Jesus limits his power and finally destroys him (verses 2,7,10).

Jesus' closing words to the spiritually rich at Smyrna summarize the comfort he has already offered. To trust that God limits evil for our good and to believe amid troubles that Jesus always triumphs over the devil—that's what it means to be faithful. In Greek, as in English, the word *faithful* comes from the word *faith*. Although Jesus uses the plural in the first half of verse 10 to warn them that the devil will put some of them in prison, he reverts to the singular "you" in the command to be faithful. Christians may be persecuted in groups, but each person must believe for himself or herself.

The invitation to faith is in the form of a command: Carry this trust to your grave! "Be faithful, even to the point of death, and I will give you the crown of life" (verse 10). The crown stands both for royalty and for reward. Crowns were worn by conquering kings and victorious athletes. A literal translation of Jesus' promise reads, "the crown of *the* life."

The Christian's reward for lifetime faithfulness is the only life that really counts, eternal life. The Savior's solid promise makes this Bible passage a favorite at Lutheran confirmations.

This letter ends, as the other six do, with a plea and a promise (verse 11). The plea is to hear, and the promise is paired with verse 10's invitation to faithfulness. "He who overcomes" reminds us of the crown that belongs to the victor. The one who has the crown of eternal life will not be hurt by "the second death." This promise to the church at Smyrna helps us understand chapter 20, verse 6: "The second death has no power over them, but they will be priests of God and of Christ and will reign with him for a thousand years." The second death is the end of grace for the unbeliever. It begins at physical death and extends to eternal suffering. The thousand years is the New Testament age. During this time believers live and serve Christ with the conviction that not even death will separate them from their Savior.

The third letter: to Pergamum

¹²"To the angel of the church in Pergamum write:

These are the words of him who has the sharp, double-edged sword. ¹³I know where you live—where Satan has his throne. Yet you remain true to my name. You did not renounce your faith in me, even in the days of Antipas, my faithful witness, who was put to death in your city— where Satan lives.

¹⁴Nevertheless, I have a few things against you: You have people there who hold to the teaching of Balaam, who taught Balak to entice the Israelites to sin by eating food sacrificed to idols and by committing sexual immorality. ¹⁵Likewise you also have those who hold to the teaching of the Nicolaitans. ¹⁶Repent therefore! Otherwise,

I will soon come to you and will fight against them with the sword of my mouth.

¹⁷He who has an ear, let him hear what the Spirit says to the churches. To him who overcomes, I will give some of the hidden manna. I will also give him a white stone with a new name written on it, known only to him who receives it.

Pergamum was a thriving city north of Smyrna. At one time the Roman provincial government was located there. During that period Pergamum attracted travelers and trade and grew to a size rivaling Ephesus and Smyrna.

John records Jesus' command for him to write to the congregation at Pergamum. When the angel, or pastor, at Pergamum reads this letter to the congregation, they will know that what they are hearing is from their Savior.

Jesus identifies himself to the church at Pergamum as the one "who has the sharp, double-edged sword" (verse 12). This is the same picture he used at the beginning of the vision of the seven letters (1:16). The congregation at Pergamum should accept what they are about to hear as the Word of God's Son. The sharpness of a sword is its effectiveness. Through Isaiah God said, "My word that goes out from my mouth . . . will . . . achieve the purpose for which I sent it" (Isaiah 55:11). The double edge cuts both ways: the law criticizes; the gospel comforts. The church at Pergamum will feel both edges of this sword in this letter from Jesus.

"I know where you live" (verse 13), Jesus said. Just as he knew the deeds of the Ephesians (2:2) and the poverty of the church at Smyrna (2:9), the Lord's fiery, blazing eyes (1:14) saw what was happening at Pergamum. This was a comforting thought for the members of this church. Jesus knew how hard it was for them to remain true to him in a city where Satan had his throne. A throne is a seat of power. Satan was especially influential in Pergamum. The Roman government promoted emperor worship. The Greeks worshipped Zeus with sacrifices and sexually immoral rites. These pagan pressures had drawn away some members of the congregation (verse 14). Besides that, Satan raised up the false teachings of the Nicolaitans there (verse 15), as he had in Ephesus (2:6).

Jesus saw what the believers in Pergamum had to face. He commends them for remaining true to his name (verse 13). Jesus' name is his reputation. His name is "everything" he has commanded us to learn about him and teach others (Matthew 28:20). His message of salvation brings people to kneel before him in faith: "At the name of Jesus, every knee should bow" (Philippians 2:10). The Christians at Pergamum had defended Jesus' good name by holding tightly to his teachings.

The faith of the faithful had been put to the test in Pergamum. One of their members was put to death for holding tightly to the teachings of Jesus. The English word *martyr* comes from the Greek word Jesus uses in verse 13 for witness. Because they held to Jesus' double-edged Word—his teachings, his name—many of the early believers, such as Stephen (Acts 7:54-60), were martyred and by their death gave a powerful witness for their Lord.

At Pergamum the martyr's name was Antipas. In all recorded history, his name is mentioned only here. Yet to have the epitaph "faithful witness" is a greater honor to a believer than a flattering column on an obituary page. Three things hint at the horrible circumstances surrounding his death. "Even in the days of Antipas" (verse 13) suggests that this event was especially trying for the congregation. So remarkable was Antipas' witness and martyrdom that the congregation still remembered it as "the days of Antipas." Also, the vicious nature of the attack on him showed that Satan had made the city his base of operations.

Following the pattern of five of the seven letters, Jesus follows his commendation of the congregation with warnings about some weaknesses that persist there. Jesus has "a few things" (verse 14) against them. Although he must point out sin, the gracious heart of the Savior does not characterize the whole church with the sins of a few. He mentions their strengths first and does not exaggerate their weaknesses. By this, Jesus models the way Christians should deal with one another.

The "few things" Jesus had against them included false living and false teaching. Members who got involved in the pagan sacrifice rituals of their society were imitating sins Israel committed during the days of Moses. Although Balak, the Moabite king, was not able to get the diviner Balaam to curse Israel outright (Numbers 22–24), Balaam "taught Balak to entice the Israelites to sin by eating food sacrificed to idols and by committing sexual immorality" (verse 14). Balak, who could not defeat Israel with a direct approach, weakened them by appealing to their lusts.

The same things happened at Pergamum. In public the congregation gave a bold witness and defense of the name of Jesus. But some of the members privately caved in to the sins of the pagans, who sought fertile fields and material profit from their false gods by sacrificing animals and engaging in sexual intercourse with temple prostitutes. It was an attractive worship formula: win the gods' favor while indulging your own lusts. Although we know little about the Nicolaitans (see verse 6), their teachings were probably compatible with pagan idolatry and adultery.

Notice how Jesus words his warnings against the weaknesses at Pergamum: "You have people there . . ." and "Likewise you also have those . . ." (verses 14,15). There is an accusatory tone that considers the whole congregation complicit in these sins to the extent that they tolerate them. Very quickly, then, follows, "Repent therefore!" (verse 16). Repentance is the Savior's call for a 180-degree turn of heart. The congregation must turn from this sin and sinful toleration of it and turn back in trust to Jesus' forgiveness.

Failure to repent will have its consequences. At the beginning of the letter, Jesus introduced himself as the one with a sharp, double-edged sword in his mouth (verse 12). Now he threatens to use this power against the unrepentant. The source of all false living is false teaching. So, when the sharp, effective Word from Jesus' mouth attacks "the teaching of Balaam" (verse 14) and "the teaching of the Nicolaitans" (verse 15), the practices will be destroyed along with the sinful practitioners. Jesus threatened that this judgment would occur "soon" (verse 16). If the sword of God's Word is not heeded, we soon die and fall under its final judgment.

"He who has an ear" (verse 17) is a pointed way of getting everyone's attention. It is the Lord's way of saying, "Every single one of you must listen to what the Spirit says to the churches." In this congregation plagued by false teaching, Jesus points to divine inspiration in three ways. His command to John to write shows that these words are not by a human author. The sword of his mouth is mentioned twice, in verses 12 and 16. Here Jesus says that his words are "what the Spirit says." Jesus taught his disciples that the Holy Spirit's witness coincides with his own: "The Holy Spirit . . . will teach you all things and will remind you of everything I have said to you" (John 14:26).

The closing follows the pattern of the letters before and after this one. The believer who remains faithful to Jesus is called the one "who overcomes" (verse 17). Then a gospel promise, uniquely worded for each church, is added to the urgent appeal to listen to the Spirit. Pergamum receives the promise of hidden manna and a white stone. The manna is Jesus and all he did to win eternal life for us. "For the bread of God is he who comes down from heaven and gives life to the world" (John 6:33). To eat this manna means to believe the gospel message of Jesus. This gospel and its reward of eternal life are hidden from those whose false pride claims a better avenue to God (Matthew 13:11; 1 Corinthians 2:9; Colossians 3:2,3). Jesus prayed, "I praise you, Father, Lord of heaven and earth, because you have hidden these things from the wise and learned, and revealed them to little children" (Matthew 11:25).

The gospel announces forgiveness. Those who trust this gospel are justified by faith, that is, they are pronounced innocent. The white stone corresponds to the voting stones that juries in that part of the world used to arrive at their verdict. If they gave the judge a white stone, they indicated acquittal. They returned a guilty verdict by giving him a black stone. In the Bible a new name often signifies a new relationship with God. The white stone and the new name assure each believing heart that it has been declared innocent before God.

The fourth letter: to Thyatira

¹⁸"To the angel of the church in Thyatira write:

These are the words of the Son of God, whose eyes are like blazing fire and whose feet are like burnished bronze. ¹⁹I know your deeds, your love and faith, your service and perseverance, and that you are now doing more than you did at first.

²⁰Nevertheless, I have this against you: You tolerate that woman Jezebel, who calls herself a prophetess. By her teaching she misleads my servants into sexual immorality and the eating of food sacrificed to idols. ²¹I have given her

time to repent of her immorality, but she is unwilling. [22]So I will cast her on a bed of suffering, and I will make those who commit adultery with her suffer intensely, unless they repent of her ways. [23]I will strike her children dead. Then all the churches will know that I am he who searches hearts and minds, and I will repay each of you according to your deeds. [24]Now I say to the rest of you in Thyatira, to you who do not hold to her teaching and have not learned Satan's so-called deep secrets (I will not impose any other burden on you): [25]Only hold on to what you have until I come.

[26]To him who overcomes and does my will to the end, I will give authority over the nations—

[27] 'He will rule them with an iron scepter;
      he will dash them to pieces like pottery'—

just as I have received authority from my Father. [28]I will also give him the morning star. [29]He who has an ear, let him hear what the Spirit says to the churches.

The geographical order Jesus follows in addressing the churches of Asia Minor now turns us inland. With Ephesus, Smyrna, and Pergamum we traveled north along the coast of the Aegean Sea. Thyatira is east and a little south of Pergamum. Luke relates that Thyatira was Lydia's hometown (Acts 16:14).

Again, Jesus asked John to write down his words. In the minds of the listeners, this should remove any doubts that its message originated in the human mind. The letter is addressed to the "angel" of the church (verse 18). This angel is the messenger who regularly brought the message of Jesus to his people. Now, as pastor, he would also carry this special letter from the Savior to them.

Jesus borrows another description of himself from the beginning of the vision of the letters. The eyes "like blazing fire" and feet "like burnished bronze" (verse 18) recall the first sight John had of Jesus (1:14,15). His eyes tell us that the Lord knows all, and his feet tell us that he has the power to enforce his will. The letter that follows shows that the Lord is using his omniscient eyes and his omnipotent feet at Thyatira.

Jesus knew what was going on at Ephesus (2:2), Smyrna (2:9), and Pergamum (2:13), and his eyes see what is happening at Thyatira too. A short commendation to this church precedes (verse 19) and follows (verse 24) the long rebuke in verses 20 through 23. Jesus frames his criticism, the second longest, with words directed to the faithful. They are the ones who will listen and respond by dealing with the unrepentant sinners among them.

The church at Thyatira was growing but struggling. Jesus commended them because they were "now doing more than [they] did at first" (verse 19). His all-seeing eyes recorded not only their many good deeds but also their service and their ability to bear up under troubles. He saw into their hearts and noticed the faith and love that were behind their actions. Every congregation of believers may be sure that the Savior sees their faith and good works even when only their problems seem obvious to the world.

With the same love, but with a warning spirit, Jesus must report the negative things he sees at Thyatira. The good members there knew Jesus opposed the false teachings and horrible sexual practices in which some of their members were involved. So Jesus begins not by rebuking the heresy and immorality, but by reprimanding the "good" members for putting up with it: "I have this against you: You tolerate that woman Jezebel" (verse 20). In more direct words than he used at Pergamum (2:16), Jesus makes it clear that toleration of sin incurs the same divine anger as sin itself. James wrote about the loving duty Christians have toward their brothers and sisters in faith: "My brothers, if one of you should wander from the truth and someone should bring him back, remember this: Whoever turns a sinner from the error of his way will save him from death and cover over a multitude of sins" (James 5:19,20).

To demonstrate the seriousness of the congregation's inaction, Jesus describes the ugly sins he sees at Thyatira. Pergamum was only a few miles away, and the false teaching and sexual immorality at Thyatira seem to be much like the sins Balaam represented there (2:14). At Thyatira, however, there is a specific individual working inside the congregation to draw people away from Jesus. Jesus calls that evil influence "Jezebel" (verse 20). This was probably not her real name but a reference to the kind of influence she exerted on certain members of the church. When King Ahab married Jezebel, he imported her pagan influence to the Northern Kingdom. He allowed his new queen to set up worship centers in Israel for her false gods (1 Kings 16:31-33). In the same manner, the Jezebel at Thyatira "calls herself a prophetess" (verse 20) but does not originate from God's people. She leads them away from their worship of the true God: "By her teaching she misleads my servants" (verse 20).

Jezebel typifies church members who want the blessings they see in the church without renouncing the sins they enjoy outside it. She was a member of the congregation, an influential one, who took for herself a teaching position as prophetess. By her teaching, she tried to convince the congregation that her pagan attachments were compatible with her new Christian faith. She tried to justify her immoral actions by involving other members in sacrifices to pagan gods and fertility rituals.

On Mount Carmel, Elijah called the Israelites away from the first Jezebel: "How long will you waver between two opinions? If the LORD is God, follow him; but if Baal is God, follow him" (1 Kings 18:21). In his Sermon on the Mount, Jesus called us to the same decision: "No one can serve two masters. . . .You cannot serve both God and Money" (Matthew 6:24). Now Jesus issues the same call to the Jezebel at Thyatira: "I have given her time to repent of her immorality, but she is unwilling" (verse 21).

The blazing eyes that saw Jezebel's sins will give way to judgment from Jesus' burnished bronze feet. But the Lord will deal with the idolatry and adultery at Thyatira in a different way than he did at Pergamum. At Pergamum he fought the false teachings and practices with the sword of the Word (verse 16). But here Jesus predicts physical punishment for the unrepentant. Jezebel had already rejected the correction of the Word during the time Jesus gave her to repent. If we take the name Jezebel to be figurative, "her children" (verse 23) are not her physical offspring, but her supporters in the congregation. The punishment will fit the crime: Jesus will repay them "according to [their] deeds" (verse 23). The wording in verses 22 and 23 suggests suffering and death from sexually transmitted diseases (compare Romans 1:27).

Yet God always brings good out of evil. Signs of God's grace appear several times in this section of severe warning. While he threatens punishment in verse 22, Jesus holds out the hope that he will not have to carry out his threat: "unless they repent of her ways." Even if they do not repent and Jesus has to strike them dead, this too will work for good. The churches will be warned that Jesus has flaming eyes and bronze feet: he "searches hearts and minds" and "will repay each of [them] according to [their] deeds" (verse 23).

Another sign of grace comes at the end of the warnings. Jesus preserved some ("the rest of you in Thyatira," verse 24) who did not tolerate Jezebel's teachings or involve themselves in her immoralities. These people were not taken in by Satan's "so-called deep secrets" (verse 24). Every temptation of Satan calls God's wisdom into question. Every sin accuses God of not telling the truth. Satan is always insinuating that he knows something that God and the godly do not. The Jezebel at Thyatira lured people in the same way Satan did in Eden: "Did God really say . . . ?" (Genesis 3:1).

The believers in Thyatira will remain faithful only if they hold to the teaching of "through faith alone." Jesus imposes only one "burden" (verse 24) on any Christian: "Hold on to what you have until I come" (verse 25). This echo of 2:10, "Be faithful, even to the point of death," is reechoed by the hymnwriter: "Only believe!" (*Christian Worship* [CW] 473:2). Faith is the only real burden anyone bears for Jesus, and he assures us, "My yoke is easy and my burden is light" (Matthew 11:30).

The one who holds on to what he has will be the one "who overcomes" (verse 26). Jesus adds that those who overcome do his will "to the end" (verse 26). Of course, this cannot mean that their lives will be without sin. It means that "faith by itself, if it is not accompanied by action, is dead" (James 2:17). The lives of those who overcome will be characterized by doing God's will. When they sin, their faith responds to each new call to repentance, and new fruits suitable for repentance appear.

To the victor go the spoils. The victors at Thyatira will receive authority over the nations (verse 27). Authority over nations was prophesied for Jesus in Psalm 2:9 and fulfilled when he received authority from his Father after his resurrection. This authority is his to give to his faithful followers. He promised, "When the Son of Man sits on his glorious throne, you who have followed me will also sit on twelve thrones, judging the twelve tribes of Israel" (Matthew 19:28).

VS 26 & 27 NOT REALLY ADDRESSED!

43

The imagery of Psalm 2 recalls the burnished bronze feet of Jesus in the introduction of this letter (2:18). The bronze feet, the iron scepter, and the smashed pottery picture the physical power Jesus exercises on behalf of his church. "God placed all things under his feet and appointed him to be head over everything for the church" (Ephesians 1:22). But he also uses this power to carry out his will against those who do not respond to the persuasive power of his Word. While these words bring comfort to the faithful at Thyatira, they warn the unrepentant that, one way or the other, Jesus' will must be done.

Jesus also promises to give "the morning star" (verse 28). This word picture is explained in chapter 22, verse 16. There Jesus says that he is "the bright Morning Star." Thus this is a promise to give himself. The star is every blessing found in Christ: forgiveness, victory, authority to judge the nations, eternal life in the presence of God.

While in the first three letters an urgent call to hear preceded the promise, in this letter the call to hear comes after the promise (verse 29). The sharp warnings in this letter as well as the commendations and promises come from the same Spirit who speaks to all the churches. Every church should listen to his inspired words.

The fifth letter: to Sardis

3 "To the angel of the church in Sardis write:

These are the words of him who holds the seven spirits of God and the seven stars. I know your deeds; you have a reputation of being alive, but you are dead. ²Wake up! Strengthen what remains and is about to die, for I have not found your deeds complete in the sight of my God. ³Remember, therefore, what you have received and heard;

obey it, and repent. But if you do not wake up, I will come like a thief, and you will not know at what time I will come to you.

⁴Yet you have a few people in Sardis who have not soiled their clothes. They will walk with me, dressed in white, for they are worthy. ⁵He who overcomes will, like them, be dressed in white. I will never blot out his name from the book of life, but will acknowledge his name before my Father and his angels. ⁶He who has an ear, let him hear what the Spirit says to the churches.

The command to write that Jesus gave John in chapter 1, verse 19, is repeated at the beginning of each of the seven letters to the churches. This is not simple repetition to maintain a pattern. It emphasizes Jesus' personal concern for each church and its angel, or pastor. Each congregation receives the words of its letter as a personal, inspired message of the Lord of the church.

Sardis is the fifth of the seven churches. The order of the seven letters follows a geographical pattern that traveled north from Ephesus to Smyrna and Pergamum, along the Aegean coastline. With the fourth letter to Thyatira (2:18) we moved inland, to the east. Now, with the letter to Sardis, we begin moving south. Sardis is almost directly east of Smyrna (see map on page vi).

Jesus presents himself to the congregation at Sardis as the one "who holds the seven spirits of God and the seven stars" (3:1). This is a variation of his introduction in the letter to the Ephesians, where he describes himself as the one who holds the seven stars and walks among the seven golden lampstands (2:1). The seven spirits signify the Holy Spirit. In chapter 1, verse 4, John mentioned "the seven spirits before his throne" between his reference to the Father and the Son. We confess in the Nicene Creed that the Holy Spirit proceeds from the Father and the Son. Although Jesus introduces himself as the author at the beginning of each letter, every letter ends with the reminder to "hear what the Spirit says to the churches" (2:7,11,17,29; 3:6,13,22). It is the work of the Holy Spirit to confirm the message of Jesus. Jesus told his disciples, "The Holy Spirit, whom the Father will send in my name, will teach you all things and will remind you of everything I have said to you" (John 14:26).

The seven stars Jesus holds are the pastors of the seven churches. Jesus already explained that "the seven stars are the angels of the seven churches" (1:20). These human messengers of the Word are held by the same hands that hold the divine messenger of the Word, the Holy Spirit. What Sardis hears—what every Christian congregation hears!—are the words of Jesus, inspired by his Spirit, communicated by his pastors.

The omniscient Jesus says, "I know your deeds" (verse 1). At Ephesus and Thyatira these words were followed by commendation for spiritual accomplishments, but not here. The deeds of the congregation at Sardis only served to perpetuate a good reputation that was unearned. "You have a reputation for being alive, but you are dead" (verse 1). Congregations may gain a lively image with full pews, big budgets, impressive buildings, a high community profile, influential members, much activity. Whether Sardis' lively reputation was in their own community or among the other churches, we don't know. But "the LORD does not look at the things man looks at. Man looks at the outward appearance, but the LORD looks at the heart" (1 Samuel 16:7). Jesus judges a church's liveliness by each member's strength of faith. He told the people at Sardis, "I have not found your deeds complete in the sight of my God" (verse 2). As faith without works is dead, so works without faith are hypocrisy.

Out of seven churches, Sardis and Laodicea are the only two that were not bothered by persecution or false doctrine. Yet both suffered from internal spiritual decay that had reached advanced stages. They responded to external peace with internal apathy. This fact should remind us that God may permit trouble in our personal lives and congregations for loving purposes. With this trust Paul wrote, "We also rejoice in our sufferings" (Romans 5:3). Peter urges his suffering readers, "Rejoice that you participate in the sufferings of Christ" (1 Peter 4:13).

Self-satisfaction usually accompanies spiritual deadness. Paul warned the Corinthians, "If you think you are standing firm, be careful that you don't fall!" (1 Corinthians 10:12). Jesus warned the church at Sardis, "Wake up! Strengthen what remains and is about to die" (verse 2). Jesus' wake-up call is a call to repentance. Sardis must admit that their spiritual inertia is just as faith-destroying as false doctrine and immoral living.

"What remains" (verse 3) at Sardis is a little bit of faith. That faith can be renewed and strengthened only by the Word of the Savior. "Faith comes from hearing the message, and the message is heard through the word of Christ" (Romans 10:17). Now we can better understand why Jesus introduced himself to Sardis as the author of the Word, the Spirit as divine carrier, and the pastor as messenger. "Remember, therefore, what you have received and heard; obey it, and repent" (verse 3). Christian congregations will view every sort of trouble as a chastening reminder to return to the Word.

Failure to repent always brings dire consequences. For the Ephesians it was the removal of their lampstand (2:5). For the church in Pergamum it was the double-edged sword of the Word (2:16); at Thyatira, physical suffering and death (2:22,23). At Sardis the threat to the unrepentant is the unexpected coming of Jesus in judgment. Jesus had issued this warning before: "Therefore keep watch, because you do not know on what day your Lord will come" (Matthew 24:42; see also 25:13). Whether Jesus returns when we die or at the final judgment, spiritual apathy will make his return as unexpected as that of a "thief" in the night (Matthew 24:43).

Most of the members at Sardis were living off their reputation. Their flickering faith held on to "what remains" (verse 2). They had to search their memories for what they had "received and heard" (verse 3). Only "a few people in Sardis" remained strong (verse 4). Note that Jesus says they "have not soiled their clothes" (verse 4). This is a remarkable statement in view of the fact that Jesus has mentioned no specific immorality or false teaching at Sardis. The sin by which the majority dirtied their clothes was apathy and indifference toward their Savior. This warning applies to every member in churches with the best reputations: "Examine yourselves to see whether you are in the faith; test yourselves" (2 Corinthians 13:5).

White clothes are a symbol of perfection. Clean clothing always refers to what the believers receive from their Savior. It represents the righteous life of Jesus credited to us through faith (Romans 4:3-5). Isaiah wrote about his confidence in this holiness: "[God] has clothed me with garments of salvation and arrayed me in a robe of righteousness" (Isaiah 61:10). In verse 5 the white clothes the believers in Sardis wear were given to them. It was not something they made for themselves: "He who overcomes will . . . be dressed in white" (verse 5). Although "all our righteous acts are like filthy rags" (Isaiah 64:6), believers wear white clothes because "they have washed their robes and made them white in the blood of the Lamb" (Revelation 7:14).

Those who wear the white clothes of Jesus' blood and righteousness have their name written in the book of life (verse 5). The certainty of eternal election is bolstered by Jesus' promise: "I will never blot out his name from the book of life" (verse 5). The Father chose us for Jesus' sake in eternity (Ephesians 1:4). That's the reason Jesus assures us, "My Father, who has given them to me, is greater than all; no one can snatch them out of my Father's hand" (John 10:29).

The book of life symbolizes God's record of the elect. The psalmist writes that the names of those erased from this book lose their eternal salvation: "Do not let them share in your salvation. May they be blotted out of the book of life and not be listed with the righteous" (Psalm 69:27,28; compare Exodus 32:32). Those who are recorded in the book are assured of an eternity with God: "At that time your people—everyone whose name is found written in the book—will be delivered" (Daniel 12:1). The book of life is mentioned throughout Revelation (13:8; 17:8; 20:12; 21:27).

Jesus will "acknowledge" the elect in front of his Father and the angels (verse 5). Our Lord will not quietly admit that he knows us. "Acknowledge" means to give a formal, public testimony to the names of believers. Jesus' acknowledgment of the elect will give recognition to their faith in him. Jesus said, "Whoever acknowledges me before men, I will also acknowledge him before my Father in heaven" (Matthew 10:32). To those who did not confess their faith on earth, Jesus will say on the Last Day, "I never knew you" (Matthew 7:23).

This letter closes with another urgent appeal to hear what the Holy Spirit is saying to the congregation at Sardis.

The sixth letter: to Philadelphia

7"To the angel of the church in Philadelphia write:

These are the words of him who is holy and true, who holds the key of David. What he opens no one can shut, and what he shuts no one can open. [8]I know your deeds. See, I have placed before you an open door that no one can shut. I know that you have little strength, yet you have kept my word and have not denied my name. [9]I will make those who are of the synagogue of Satan, who claim to be Jews though they are not, but are liars—I will make them come and fall down at your feet and acknowledge that I have loved you. [10]Since you have kept my command to endure patiently, I will also keep you from the hour of trial that is going to come upon the whole world to test those who live on the earth.

[11]I am coming soon. Hold on to what you have, so that no one will take your crown. [12]Him who overcomes I will make a pillar in the temple of my God. Never again will he leave it. I will write on him the name of my God and the name of the city of my God, the new Jerusalem, which is coming down out of heaven from my God; and I will also write on him my new name. [13]He who has an ear, let him hear what the Spirit says to the churches.

Among the seven churches of Asia Minor, Philadelphia and Smyrna are the only two who receive no criticism from Jesus. They are the faithful churches. Philadelphia lies southeast of Sardis, about 150 miles inland from the Aegean Sea (see map on page vi). The city exists today and has a number of Christian congregations.

Jesus commands John to write down the letter and then introduces himself. In five earlier introductions, Jesus borrowed descriptions of himself from the opening of the vision of the seven letters (1:12-20). This time he adds to it. By calling himself "holy and true" (verse 7), Jesus is addressing the opposition the congregation at Philadelphia faced from the Jews (verse 9). Jesus is "the LORD, your God, the Holy One of Israel, your Savior" (Isaiah 43:3). "True" means genuine and authentic. In spite of Jewish doubts and accusations, Jesus is the promised Messiah.

The holy and true Messiah holds the "key of David" (verse 7). The Jews at Philadelphia would recognize the meaning of this Old Testament reference. Eliakim was given the key that opened David's storehouse and thus received the right to dispense the temporal blessings of God's Old Testament kingdom (see Isaiah 22:22). Eliakim serves as a type of Christ. The victorious Christ holds the key of David, which in his case represents the right to dispense the blessings of God's kingdom of grace—forgiveness of sins and eternal life.

The "keys of death and Hades" mentioned earlier (1:18) and the "keys of the kingdom of heaven" (Matthew 16:19) are the same as the "key of David," only viewed from a different standpoint. All refer to the power to determine eternal destinies. Jesus, not Satan, has the power over death, a power he gained by his death and resurrection. When people believe his message of grace, he opens heaven to them. And no one can shut the door against them. If they refuse to believe, they separate themselves from him and remain under the curse of sin and eternal death. And none of those people can open the door to heaven, for Jesus has closed and locked it against them.

Jesus had compassion on the church at Philadelphia. "I know your deeds," he assures them (verse 8). The detailed lists of Christian actions attributed to Ephesus (2:2,3), Smyrna (2:9), Pergamum (2:13), and Thyatira (2:19) are missing here. Philadelphia did not share Sardis' reputation as a going and growing church. In the eyes of the Savior, however, Philadelphia had the one thing needful. Jesus told them, "You have kept my word" (verse 8) and "you have kept my command to endure patiently" (verse 10). Not memorable deeds, but faith and faithfulness characterize this church.

Among the seven letters, Jesus' commendation of Philadelphia takes a unique form. Instead of making a list of what they did for him, Jesus offers many promises of what he will do for them. He will give them an open door (verse 8). He will work through them to lead their Jewish opponents to know his love (verse 9), and he will keep them from the "hour of trial" that is coming (verse 10).

The open door reminds us that Jesus holds the keys of David. He holds the door of heaven open for believers and commissions them to open that door for others. The description of the false Jewish element at Philadelphia is almost identical to the one at Smyrna (see 2:9). The Lord assured the church at Smyrna that he would keep them through their troubles, but he promises more to Philadelphia. To the promise of an open door he adds this prophecy: "I will make them come and fall down at your feet and acknowledge that I have loved you" (verse 9). Jesus will let the Philadelphians see the fruits of their faithful gospel witness. His promise can be understood in two ways. Either their detractors will be won over by the Word they share, or they will be forced to give up their opposition when they see how God keeps them firm against their attacks.

The church at Philadelphia demonstrated a love for God's Word and a desire to share it with others. Those twin strengths characterize every faithful Christian congregation.

The NIV translates verse 10, "Since you have kept my command to endure patiently." Literally, Jesus said, "Since you have kept my Word of patience." Jesus was talking about the power of his Word to make them patient, not their obedience to his command to be patient. The sense of his message is, "You have held on to my patience-creating Word." This understanding of his words coincides with Paul's statement about the power of the Word: "For everything that was written in the past was written to teach us, so that through endurance and the encouragement of the Scriptures we might have hope" (Romans 15:4).

Jesus will spare the faithful in Philadelphia "the hour of trial" (verse 10) that is coming. The hour indicates a limited, relatively short period of time. God graciously limits how long temptations can afflict his people. Jesus said, "If those days had not been cut short, no one would survive, but for the sake of the elect those days will be shortened" (Matthew 24:22).

This hour of trial will "come upon the whole world" and it will test everybody who lives on earth (verse 10). So keeping the Philadelphians from the hour of trial cannot mean they will be taken out of this world before the final judgment. Some who teach that God will "rapture" believers out of this world before the last days cite this passage as evidence of that teaching. The word "keep" (verse 10) means "protect." Jesus will not remove them from the world but will protect them from the temptations of the last days.

The Savior adds another promise: "I am coming soon" (verse 11). These words have a tone different from his words to Sardis: "I will come like a thief" (3:3). That was a threat. For the Philadelphians, Jesus' return is a promise that their patient endurance will soon be rewarded. For all the faithful everywhere, Jesus repeats this promise at the end of the book: "Yes, I am coming soon" (22:20).

Because he is coming soon, Jesus urged Thyatira (see 2:25) and then Philadelphia (3:11), "Hold on to what you have." But the faithful congregations Philadelphia and Smyrna are promised the "crown" (verse 11). This is the crown of eternal life (see 2:10). "Him who overcomes" (verse 12) is literally one word, "victor," or "winner." The faithful will be "pillars" of the temple in heaven (see verse 12). Peter, James, and John are called pillars of the church on earth (Galatians 2:9). Here, however, pillars denote not prominence or role, but a permanent place in God's temple. A victor in heaven is like a pillar in an earthly temple: "Never again will he leave it" (verse 12).

Three times in verse 12 Jesus refers to God as "my God." These words make him a brother to those for whom he won the victory by taking on their human nature. Jesus is speaking according to his human nature when he calls the Father "my God." He spoke about himself this way before: "I am returning to my Father and your Father, to my God and your God" (John 20:17). On occasion Paul also wrote about Jesus in this way: "The head of Christ is God" (1 Corinthians 11:3; see also 15:27,28).

Our most personal identification is our name. We receive God's name when we are reborn into his family by our baptism "in the name of the Father and of the Son and of the Holy Spirit" (Matthew 28:19). The name of the holy city is the new home address for those who wear God's name. When Jesus finished his suffering, "God exalted him to the highest place and gave him the name that is above every name" (Philippians 2:9). His new name is his new reputation, not as sufferer, but as victor. Jesus gives this new name and reputation to everyone who overcomes with him.

The pointed encouragement for everyone at Philadelphia to listen to the words of the Spirit has no sharp edges. It is purely a word of comfort. Jesus calls them people who "have kept my word" (verse 8) and "have kept my command to endure patiently" (verse 10). Our Lord's last word to the faithful in Philadelphia is like Paul's plea on behalf of the Philippians: "This is my prayer: that your love may abound more and more in knowledge and depth of insight, so that you may be able to discern what is best and may be pure and blameless until the day of Christ" (Philippians 1:9,10).

The seventh letter: to Laodicea

¹⁴"To the angel of the church in Laodicea write:

These are the words of the Amen, the faithful and true witness, the ruler of God's creation. ¹⁵I know your deeds, that you are neither cold nor hot. I wish you were either one or the other! ¹⁶So, because you are lukewarm—neither hot nor cold—I am about to spit you out of my mouth. ¹⁷You say, 'I am rich; I have acquired wealth and do not need a thing.' But you do not realize that you are wretched, pitiful, poor, blind and naked. ¹⁸I counsel you to buy from me gold refined in the fire, so you can become rich; and white clothes to wear, so you can cover your shameful nakedness; and salve to put on your eyes, so you can see.

¹⁹Those whom I love I rebuke and discipline. So be earnest, and repent. ²⁰Here I am! I stand at the door and knock. If anyone hears my voice and opens the door, I will come in and eat with him, and he with me.

²¹To him who overcomes, I will give the right to sit with me on my throne, just as I overcame and sat down with my Father on his throne. ²²He who has an ear, let him hear what the Spirit says to the churches.

The order of the churches addressed in the seven letters of the vision has proceeded clockwise around the western region of Asia Minor. First we went north along the Aegean coastline, then inland and south. Laodicea is the southernmost of the seven churches and about 160 miles east of Ephesus (see map on page vi). Colossae is not far from Laodicea, and Paul mentions the Laodiceans four times in his epistle to the Colossians. Paul also wrote a letter to the Laodiceans at one time (Colossians 4:16), but it is not preserved in the inspired Scriptures. Laodicea enjoyed fellowship with two nearby Christian congregations and some considerable attention from Missionary Paul.

Jesus directed John to write to the pastor, or "angel," at Laodicea (verse 14). As God's messenger, this pastor bears responsibility for the poor spiritual condition Jesus attributes to this church. James wrote, "We who teach will be judged more strictly" (James 3:1). Yet behind the hard words of this letter, we can see the Lord's heart of love: "Those whom I love I rebuke and discipline" (verse 19). It will be the pastor's work to lay the law and gospel of this letter on the hearts of his people.

As in the previous six letters, Jesus introduces himself in a way that hints at the content of the letter to follow. "The Amen, the faithful and true witness" (verse 14) is writing to a lukewarm, unfaithful church. Laodicea has not been a true witness to Jesus. The word *amen* derives from the Hebrew word for truth. In the Old Testament God calls himself the "God of truth" (Isaiah 65:16). In the New Testament Jesus calls himself "the way and the truth and the life" (John 14:6). Jesus is more than the content of a truthful message. He is a faithful communicator of the truth to his people. His actions are always consistent with what he says. In chapter 19, verse 11, Jesus is also called "Faithful and True." "True" means authentic. Since Jesus comes from God, his witness to the truth is genuine: "I am telling you what I have seen in the Father's presence" (John 8:38). All these descriptions of Jesus sharply contrast with the nature of the congregation to which he is writing.

The final description Jesus offers of himself is "the ruler of God's creation." This too hints at the weakness in Laodicea.

This congregation put false confidence in created things. They were comfortable and felt protected by their wealth. They need to know right from the start that the one who is speaking to them stands higher than the created world. He can provide a security they can never find in material riches.

There is no commendation for Laodicea. Even Sardis, which Jesus said was "dead" (3:1), had "a few people" (3:4) who were faithful. But at Laodicea the judgment of the all-knowing Jesus applies to the whole congregation: "You are neither cold nor hot. . . .You are lukewarm" (verses 15,16). No outside persecution or inside pressure from false teachers was there. Laodicea suffered from disinterest and material self-satisfaction.

The severity of their spiritual condition could not be exaggerated. Jesus wished they were either hot or cold. If they were burning with dedication, there would be no question about the strength of their faith. "Cold" does not mean that Jesus wishes they would lose what little faith they had. It means the cold heart of someone who never came to faith. If they were frozen in unbelief, they might, at least, welcome the warmth of the gospel in contrast to their condition.

As it is, indifference has numbed their ability to respond to the truth of the gospel. "Lukewarm" means slightly heated. In context it does not mean halfway between hot and cold. It actually means that their faith is declining from what it first was. They are on their way down, close to cold. Such lapsing faith is unpalatable to the Savior's taste: "I am about to spit you out of my mouth" (verse 16).

Jesus threatened judgment like this before. At the end of the parable of the rich fool, he said, "This is how it will be with anyone who stores up things for himself but is not rich toward God" (Luke 12:21). This is an accurate description of the Laodiceans. The externals of church life and personal wealth replaced the spiritual riches of repentance and faith. It is very hard for people who live with material comforts to believe that God is not happy with them. That's why Jesus said, "It is easier for a camel to go through the eye of a needle than for a rich man to enter the kingdom of God" (Luke 18:25). Physical comfort blunts the spiritual discomfort needed in repentance. That's why the Laodiceans did not realize that they were "wretched, pitiful, poor, blind and naked" (verse 17).

So that they can "become rich" (verse 18)—spiritually rich—Jesus urges them to make three different forms of investment. He tells them to buy "gold," "white clothes," and "salve" (verse 18). All three purchases Jesus recommends represent the riches of the gospel, but there is some divine sarcasm here that cuts through the Laodiceans' false material comfort. A government mint, the sale of fine clothing, and the manufacture of a special salve were important sources of Laodicea's economic wealth. But Jesus offers greater riches in the gospel than they will find in Laodicea's economy. Unlike the purest gold, the gospel has absolutely no impurities because it is "refined in the fire" (verse 18). Forgiveness is better than rich apparel because it offers the "white clothes" of the Savior's righteousness (verse 18; see 3:4,5). The Word of God provides better healing than the locally sold salve because it relieves spiritual blindness.

The angry Jesus who introduced himself and reproved Laodicea at the beginning of the letter now reveals his prevailing character of grace. "Those whom I love I rebuke and discipline" (verse 19). Believers frequently need the assurance that "the Lord disciplines those he loves" (Hebrews 12:6). The Laodiceans were unchallenged by persecution and false doctrine and had grown soft with wealth. They needed the rebuke and discipline of their Savior's criticism.

The "angel," or pastor, of this church must not downplay Jesus' rebuke for fear of offending the wealthy and influential. If he does, he will destroy its loving purpose. Jesus wants his rebuke to lead the Laodiceans to "be earnest, and repent" (verse 19; see also 2:5).

Verse 20 portrays the power of the gospel to invite and convert. Most of us treasure the beautiful painting of Jesus standing at the door of the believer's heart and knocking. Saving faith is not a decision the believer makes to open the door to his Savior. Jesus told his disciples, "You did not choose me, but I chose you" (John 15:16). The Laodiceans fell away from faith on their own, but the Savior took the initiative to bring them back. Not only does Jesus "stand at the door and knock" (verse 20), his "voice" is what leads us to open the door (verse 20). Paul reminded the Ephesians that this voice of truth at the door to their hearts brought them to faith: "You also were included in Christ when you heard the word of truth, the gospel of your salvation" (Ephesians 1:13).

All seven letters to the churches end with a promise. Even this letter to the lukewarm includes two promises. During their lifetimes, those who respond to the gospel's knocking will enjoy having Jesus as a dinner guest in their heart (verse 20). The picture of Jesus and the believer dining together does not suggest the Lord's Supper, because in the Lord's Supper only the believer partakes. This is instead a happy picture of those who are "at home" with Jesus during their lives on earth. Of those who were grafted to him by faith, Jesus said, "I have called you friends" (John 15:15). Jesus made this promise to all believers: "If anyone loves me, he will obey my teaching. My Father will love him, and we will come to him and make our home with him" (John 14:23).

A lifetime friend of Jesus is one "who overcomes" (verse 21). For the victors the promise of the life to come also applies. Jesus pictures eternal life as "the right to sit with me on my throne" (verse 21). John mentions God's throne 40 times in Revelation. A throne usually brings to mind the power of God (see 4:9-11). But God's throne is also a place of grace shared by the Lamb of God (22:3) who shepherds his people (7:17). The Holy Spirit is also at the throne (see 1:4) and from there offers the grace of his Word to the churches (verse 22).

In verse 21 "throne" seems to emphasize God's grace more than his power. Heaven is a gift of grace. Jesus says he "will give the right to sit" with him on the throne (verse 21). The throne in this verse is a place of reward. Jesus was rewarded with his throne after he "overcame" to win our salvation (verse 21). Now he rewards those who claim his victory through faith in him.

A church preoccupied with money and surrounded by creature comforts must open its ears to the Spirit's Word. Jesus held out hope for repentance at Laodicea and offered gracious promises to those who would respond. Yet the content of the letter as a whole gives the closing plea for open ears a somber tone. The pastor at Laodicea has a big job ahead of him. He would do well to listen to what Paul told a young pastor named Timothy: "Command those who are rich in this present world not to be arrogant nor to put their hope in wealth, which is so uncertain, but to put their hope in God. . . . In this way they will lay up treasure for themselves as a firm foundation for the coming age, so that they may take hold of the life that is truly life" (1 Timothy 6:17,19). These are fitting words for a dead church.

VISION OF THE SCROLL
(4:1–7:17)

John approaches the throne

4 After this I looked, and there before me was a door standing open in heaven. And the voice I had first heard speaking to me like a trumpet said, "Come up here, and I will show you what must take place after this." ²At once I was in the Spirit, and there before me was a throne in heaven with someone sitting on it. ³And the one who sat there had the appearance of jasper and carnelian. A rainbow, resembling an emerald, encircled the throne. ⁴Surrounding the throne were twenty-four other thrones, and seated on them were twenty-four elders. They were dressed in white and had crowns of gold on their heads. ⁵From the throne came flashes of lightning, rumblings and peals of thunder. Before the throne, seven lamps were blazing. These are the seven spirits of God. ⁶Also before the throne there was what looked like a sea of glass, clear as crystal.

In the center, around the throne, were four living creatures, and they were covered with eyes, in front and in back. ⁷The first living creature was like a lion, the second was like an ox, the third had a face like a man, the fourth was like a flying eagle. ⁸Each of the four living creatures had six wings and was covered with eyes all around, even under his wings. Day and night they never stop saying:

> "Holy, holy, holy
> is the Lord God Almighty,
> who was, and is, and is to come."

⁹Whenever the living creatures give glory, honor and thanks to him who sits on the throne and who lives for ever and ever, ¹⁰the twenty-four elders fall down before him who sits on the

*"Come up here, and I will show you
what must take place after this." (4:1)*

throne, and worship him who lives for ever and ever. They lay their crowns before the throne and say:

11 "You are worthy, our Lord and God,
  to receive glory and honor and power,
 for you created all things,
   and by your will they were created
   and have their being."

Chapter 4 introduces the second of seven visions Jesus gave to John on the isle of Patmos. In the first vision, Jesus dictated word for word the letters to the seven churches. In those seven letters John recorded language rich with symbolism. Now John begins to see visions and for the most part, he must translate into human words the divinely revealed pictures he is shown. The language becomes even more beautiful, more symbolic, and thus more difficult for us to comprehend at times.

The beginning of the second vision provides a key to understanding how all the visions relate to each other. John writes, "After this I looked . . ." (verse 1). The passing of time related by "after" refers to the passing of time in regard to the author, John, not to the events in the vision. What happens in the second and subsequent visions does not happen in historical sequence. John, of course, saw them in order, one after another. But the visions themselves pertain to many events that happen within the general time frame of the New Testament period and the judgment.

John's references to the passing of time in the last six visions prove this. The adverbs that indicate time has elapsed ("Then," 5:1; 6:1; "After this," 7:1; etc.) usually modify John's action. On occasion we will note the passing of time within a vision and from one vision to the next. But when John says, "after this I . . . ," he is talking about time that passed for him.

This understanding of the first four words of the second vision helps us understand all Revelation's visions better. Dispensationalists hold the false idea that each vision is a chapter of the church's history. John's inspired wording, however, demands that we view the visions as separate snapshots of the entire history of the church, each taken from a different angle. In other words, the visions offer different perspectives of the same events: sometimes from earth, sometimes from heaven, sometimes from hell.

Chapter 4 serves as the introduction to the last six visions. In chapters 1 to 3 John heard the voice and saw the vision of the Savior from Patmos. Now he is drawn in spirit to the doorway of heaven itself. The same trumpet voice he heard before invites him to come through the door: "Come up here, and I will show you what must take place after this" (verse 1).

The first "After this" in verse 1 was the passing of time for John. The "after this" at the end of verse 1 refers to the passing of time for the events of the vision. The events of the second and subsequent visions will take place after what Jesus revealed to John about the seven churches occurs. In chapter 1, verse 19, Jesus told John, "Write, therefore, what you have seen, what is now and what will take place later." The letter to the seven churches painted a picture of "what is now" in the church. The next six visions will show "what must take place after this" (4:1).

Millennialists use this record of John's vision of heaven to teach a rapture. By the word *rapture* they mean that God physically snatches the faithful into heaven before Jesus rules for a thousand years on earth (a millennium) in order to spare them the tribulation before the final judgment. But Jesus tells us that his reason for taking John to heaven was to show him the visions. He was not the first of many to be snatched, or raptured, in anticipation of an earthly millennium. John was an inspired scribe who went into heaven to write what Jesus told him. He returned to deliver the Revelation to the churches.

"At once," that is, as soon as Jesus invited him to come, John was "in the Spirit," according to the NIV translation (verse 2). "In spirit" is closer to the original Greek. At the end of each of the seven letters to the churches John spoke of the Holy Spirit as *the* Spirit, but here and in chapter 1, verse 10, he writes only "spirit." "In spirit" occurs again in chapter 17, verse 3, and chapter 21, verse 10. John was not physically drawn up into heaven but was "in spirit." God put him into a state of mind in which he was receptive to what Jesus was about to show him in the visions.

In front of John, in heaven, was "a throne . . . with someone sitting on it" (verse 2). In verse 3 John only briefly describes the one on the throne, without identifying him. From chapter 5, verses 1 to 6, we learn that God, including Jesus and the Holy Spirit, is on the throne. The "Holy, holy, holy" song of the living creatures in chapter 4, verse 8, confirms that verse 3 describes the triune God.

John struggles for just the exact words to express what he saw. He writes "jasper," "carnelian," and "emerald" (verse 3). Jasper is translucent like a diamond. Carnelian is a red stone. An emerald would reflect light in various colors. But we are kept from attaching symbolism to the individual stones when John writes "appearance of" and "resembling" (verse 3). John didn't see actual stones, only what looked like them.

God's indescribable glory drew John's attention first to the throne in heaven. Around God's throne are 24 elders, dressed in white and wearing gold crowns. The number 24 suggests the 12 tribes of Israel of the Old Testament and the 12 apostles of the New Testament. These elders are mentioned 12 times in the last six visions, where they frequently praise God for his salvation. The thrones they sit on Jesus promised to all believers (3:21). Thus the elders represent all believers of all times. Their white clothing is the righteousness of Christ credited to them by faith (see 3:4,5). Their gold crowns represent their rule with Jesus in eternal life (see 2:10).

John's attention again is drawn to the throne by two pictures: the lightning and thunder and the blazing lamps. These pictures help us define the brilliant glory of God described by the stones in verse 3. The picture of the lightning and thunder recalls the giving of the Ten Commandments (Exodus 19:16). John explains that the seven blazing lamps are the seven spirits of God. The seven spirits are the way Revelation speaks of the Holy Spirit (see 1:4). God sends his Holy Spirit "out into all the earth" (5:6) to announce his message of love. Together, these two pictures combine God's holiness and mercy, his justice and grace. The fact that God is "just and the one who justifies those who have faith in Jesus" (Romans 3:26) makes his glory brilliant.

In addition to the lightning and thunder and the blazing lamps, John sees "what looked like a sea of glass, clear as crystal" (verse 6) in front of the throne. His description indicates something calm, clear, and vast. Nothing outside of Revelation helps us identify this sea. John sees this glassy sea again in the fourth vision (15:2), where the believers are standing beside it. Since John includes the sea along with earlier references to God's glory, the calm, vast sea may represent the peace God's glory gives to believers. John could only record "what looked like" a sea (verse 6). Paul wrote that the peace of God "transcends all understanding" (Philippians 4:7).

The four living creatures, literally "living things," before the throne have been interpreted in various ways. John's

vision of the living creatures contains some of the symbolism that Ezekiel (Ezekiel 1) and Isaiah (Isaiah 6) used. The
living creatures in the Old Testament were angels. Because
of their wings and many eyes, many believe that John's living creatures are angels too. That is not true, however,
because John later (5:11) distinguishes between the living
creatures and the angels.

CONTRA
DICTS
BECKER

The many eyes suggest to some people that the four living creatures represent God's providence of creation. The
four creatures, however, sing two songs of praise to God
in this section (verses 8,11). Although not impossible in
vision imagery, it is unlikely that God's power or work is
singing to him. The four living creatures, then, probably do
not refer to God or to one of his attributes, such as his
power or his providence.

We notice that the lion, ox, human, and eagle faces all represent living, created beings. These living creatures seem
interested and involved in the created world. Their second
song praises God for his work of creation, not redemption
(verse 9). In chapter 6 the four living creatures invite John to
see the four horses that ride the *earth*, but they are not present for the *heavenly* events in the last three seals. The
description here and elsewhere in Revelation suggests that
the four living creatures represent all the living things in
God's creation. In that case, the eyes represent the many eyes
that look to God for his provision (Psalm 145:15; see also
Psalm 121:1; 123:1,2; Zechariah 9:1), and the wings symbolize their ability to be in the created world and yet always
before the throne of God to give him praise.

The picture of creation (the four living creatures) joining
believers (the 24 elders) to praise God is not foreign to Scripture. The psalmist wrote, "Let every creature praise his holy
name" (Psalm 145:21). The created world also has an interest

in God's saving work. Paul wrote, "The creation waits in eager expectation for the sons of God to be revealed" (Romans 8:19). That is why the elders and the living creatures join together each time they sing praise to God (verses 8-11; see also 5:8; 7:11; 19:4).

Verses 8 and 11 are really two parts to the same song. The living creatures begin and the 24 elders immediately join in (verse 10). The first part of the chant is pure praise. It glorifies God for who he is. In poetic symmetry it extols the Trinity with three verses of three. There are three "holies," three names for God, and a threefold description of his eternal nature (see 1:8).

As the elders join the four living creatures for the second verse of praise (verse 11), they lay their crowns (see verse 4) before the throne to acknowledge from whom they received them. The second verse of the song by the joint choir praises God and thanks him. The three-part poetry appears here too. "To receive glory and honor and power" means to receive praise for possessing them. The three-part closing thanks God for creating all things, creating them purposely, and sustaining their life.

The Lamb receives the scroll

5 **Then I saw in the right hand of him who sat on the throne a scroll with writing on both sides and sealed with seven seals. ²And I saw a mighty angel proclaiming in a loud voice, "Who is worthy to break the seals and open the scroll?" ³But no one in heaven or on earth or under the earth could open the scroll or even look inside it. ⁴I wept and wept because no one was found who was worthy to open the scroll or look inside. ⁵Then one of the elders said to me, "Do not weep! See, the Lion of the tribe of Judah, the Root of David, has triumphed. He is able to open the scroll and its seven seals."**

⁶Then I saw a Lamb, looking as if it had been slain, standing in the center of the throne, encircled by the four living creatures and the elders. He had seven horns and seven eyes, which are the seven spirits of God sent out into all the earth. ⁷He came and took the scroll from the right hand of him who sat on the throne. ⁸And when he had taken it, the four living creatures and the twenty-four elders fell down before the Lamb. Each one had a harp and they were holding golden bowls full of incense, which are the prayers of the saints. ⁹And they sang a new song:

> "You are worthy to take the scroll
>   and to open its seals,
> because you were slain,
>   and with your blood you purchased men for God
>   from every tribe and language and people and nation.
> ¹⁰ You have made them to be a kingdom
>   and priests to serve our God,
>   and they will reign on the earth."

¹¹Then I looked and heard the voice of many angels, numbering thousands upon thousands, and ten thousand times ten thousand. They encircled the throne and the living creatures and the elders. ¹²In a loud voice they sang:

> "Worthy is the Lamb, who was slain,
> to receive power and wealth and wisdom and strength
> and honor and glory and praise!"

¹³Then I heard every creature in heaven and on earth and under the earth and on the sea, and all that is in them, singing:

> "To him who sits on the throne and to the Lamb be praise
> and honor and glory and power, for ever and ever!"

¹⁴The four living creatures said, "Amen," and the elders fell down and worshiped.

Chapter 5 is a continuation of chapter 4's introduction to the second vision, the vision of the scroll. When John was first drawn up to heaven, he saw the glorious throne of God. His attention was diverted for a while to what he saw around the throne: the elders, the glassy sea, and the four living creatures. Now John turns back to the throne itself.

God is on the throne with a rolled up scroll in his right hand (verse 1). Scrolls were usually written on only one side, but this one had writing on both sides. Seven seals on the scroll keep it from being read. In chapters 6 and 7, after someone worthy (verse 2) is found to open the seals, the seals will be opened and the scroll will be read.

The scroll represents the future. Jesus took John into heaven in order to show him "what must take place after this" (4:1). God holds the future in his right hand. Man and created beings cannot pry into it: "No one in heaven or on earth or under the earth could open the scroll or even look inside it" (verse 3). Perhaps because he wanted to know what the future held for the struggling churches in Asia Minor, John wept when no one was able to open the scroll (verse 4).

No one in all creation has the ability to see the future. The holy angels in heaven possess vast knowledge, but they are not omniscient. The saints in heaven are holy, but they do not know how long it will be before God rescues the suffering saints on earth (6:10). On earth our limited human knowledge is further hampered by sin, and other living creatures do not have rational knowledge. The phrase "under the earth" may mean the realm of the dead or the place where Satan lives. In spite of claims by fortune-tellers and those who say they speak with the dead, Satan and the departed know nothing about the future except the certainty of their damnation. "Under the earth" may simply be the third part of the phrase to indicate the whole creation.

"One of the elders" comforted John (verse 5). "Don't weep," he said (verse 5). It makes no difference which elder spoke because all the elders, who represent all believers (see 4:4), know who is worthy to open the scroll. The believers are in heaven because they know the Savior who won the victory for them. They also know that the one who assured their future is able to know the future in every detail.

The elders refer to the one worthy to open the seals as "the Lion of the tribe of Judah, the Root of David" (verse 5). Jesus fulfilled Jacob's prophecy about Judah in Genesis 49:9,10. Jacob described the coming Messiah as a lion's cub, a lion, and a lioness and promised that "the scepter will not depart from Judah." The title "Root of David" calls to mind Isaiah's prophecy of the coming Savior. Isaiah called Jesus a shoot from the stump of Jesse and the "Root of Jesse" (Isaiah 11:1,10). Jesse was David's father, and the Gospels frequently call Jesus the son of David.

Only Jesus is able to open the seals on the scroll because only he is God. The very next thing John saw reaffirmed this truth. John saw a "Lamb, looking as if it had been slain, standing in the center of the throne" (verse 6). Thirty times Jesus appears as a lamb in Revelation. "The Lamb of God" (John 1:29) is both God and man. He stands in the center of the throne because he and the Father, although two separate persons, are one God from all eternity. Jesus became fully human in order to be slain and "[take] away the sin of the world" (John 1:29). He appears here as a victor whose work is finished. The fact that he "had been slain" (verse 6) indicates the Lamb's work for our salvation is fully accomplished. The seven horns of the Lamb symbolize his power. The Lamb who completed his work has been exalted and now has all authority in heaven and on earth.

All that we know—and all we can ever know—about the mystery of the Trinity is depicted in John's vision of the throne. Verse 1 describes one throne with one person holding the scroll. Now John sees the Lamb "in the center of the throne" (verse 6). The Lamb, in turn, possesses seven horns and seven eyes, "which are the seven spirits of God" (verse 6). John spoke of the Holy Spirit before as the seven spirits of God before the throne (1:4; 3:1; 4:5). Jesus sends the Spirit from the Father "into all the earth" (verse 6) to testify about him (John 15:26). There is only one throne, but three distinct persons occupy it.

Around the throne are those who benefit from the saving work of the Lamb, the four living creatures and the elders. The elders received their crown of eternal life from the Lamb (verse 10). The living creatures represent all creation that "will be liberated from its bondage to decay and brought into the glorious freedom of the children of God" (Romans 8:21). After the Lamb took the scroll, the believers joined all creation in a song to the Lamb.

Each of the elders and creatures carries a golden bowl of incense. John explains that these "are the prayers of the saints" (verse 8). The psalmist considered his prayers to be praise for the Savior: "May my prayer be set before you like incense" (Psalm 141:2). The harps that the elders and creatures carry indicate their preparation for singing "a new song" (verse 9). This new song, like the Psalms, is a thanksgiving to God for his work of salvation.

What the Lamb accomplished in the past determines what the future holds for believers and for all creation. The elders and the creatures know this, so they praise the Lamb for what he has done. Their new song begins by answering the angel's question, "Who is worthy?" The Lamb is worthy to open the scroll that reveals the future because, by his blood and death, he determined the future. The elders and the creatures belong to God (verse 9), they serve God (verse 10), and they will reign with him (verse 10). ON THE EARTH.

John the Baptist once proclaimed Jesus to be the Lamb of God "who takes away the sin of the world" (John 1:29). Here Jesus reveals to the apostle John that the Lamb purchased souls "from every tribe and language and people and nation" (verse 9). The four-part description symbolizes all humanity, just as the four creatures represent all living beings. Not all will be saved, but the slain Lamb has made salvation available for all. Language, race, and national origin keep no one from the Savior.

"A kingdom and priests" (verse 10) indicate the status and role that believers have already in this life (see 1:6). The Lamb made us a part of his spiritual kingdom. His kingdom "is not a matter of eating and drinking, but of righteousness, peace and joy in the Holy Spirit" (Romans 14:17). This does not refer to a thousand-year reign by force, as millenialists suggest. Those who reign in Christ's kingdom rule with the power of the Spirit's Word. They use the same Word that brought them righteousness, peace, and joy to bring others to the Lamb. God's kingdom comes when his will is done. His will is that everyone may come to faith. We rule with Christ when we are joined with him by faith.

What about the rest of verse 10 "they will reign on the earth".

Since the Lamb was slain, he already made the ultimate sacrifice for our sins. Jesus' priests, then, do not bring sacrifices to pay for their sins. They do not spend their lives trying to earn heaven. Instead, serving as his priests means giving thanks to the Lamb for earning heaven for us. Priests of the Lamb bring only "spiritual sacrifices" (1 Peter 2:5), that is, lives that glorify their Savior.

Rom 12:1

After the song by the elders and four living creatures, John saw "many angels" (verse 11). Ten thousand times ten thousand is a hundred million. These countless angels are confirmed in their holiness. Yet when it comes to matters of salvation, Peter writes, "Even angels long to look into these things" (1 Peter 1:12). The angels "encircled the throne and the living creatures and the elders" (verse 11). God assigns the angels to protect his saints and to administer his providence for all living creatures.

John hears this angelic choir singing another song of praise to the Lamb. As true God, the Lamb already possessed all "power and wealth and wisdom and strength and honor and glory and praise" (verse 12). As true man, the Lamb who was slain received all this when he rose from the dead and was exalted to God's right hand.

To complete the praise to the Lamb, another choir is added to the voices of the elders, living creatures, and angels. John heard "every creature in heaven and on earth and under the earth and on the sea" (verse 13). The word for "creature" is different from the one for "living creatures" (4:6). Since all the living creatures (literally, "living beings") in heaven and earth were already present, the creatures in this last choir are likely "created things." Even God's inanimate creation gives him praise. "The heavens declare the glory of God" (Psalm 19:1).

The worship this mass choir offers to the Lamb also praises the one sitting on the throne. The Father sent his Lamb to be our Savior. Now he gives the Lamb authority over the final judgment so "that all may honor the Son just as they honor the Father" (John 5:23). The glorious praise of God and the Lamb elicits awe from those most directly affected by their salvation, the elders and the living creatures. The living creatures said, "Amen" (verse 14), which means, "Yes, this is true!" The elders fell down and worshiped. Lying prostrate before the king was how subjects of a kingdom expressed humility and signified the king's power over them.

The Lamb opens the first four seals

The first seal: the white horse

6 **I watched as the Lamb opened the first of the seven seals. Then I heard one of the four living creatures say in a voice like thunder, "Come!" ²I looked, and there before me was a white horse! Its rider held a bow, and he was given a crown, and he rode out as a conqueror bent on conquest.**

The vision of the scroll, introduced in chapters 4 and 5, begins here. Jesus, the Lamb who is worthy, opens the first of the seven seals on the scroll (see 5:1). The first four seals of the scroll reveal four horses and their riders. These are commonly called the Four Horsemen of the Apocalypse. The symbolism of the number 4 again points to the earth. The four horses and their riders represent four influences that will affect the earth while the church waits for the triumphant return of the Lamb.

All living creatures on the earth will be affected by the things the four horsemen symbolize. So one of the four "living creatures" (see 4:6) introduces each of the horses and its rider. After the Lamb opened the first seal, John heard the thunderous voice of one of the four living creatures say, "Come!" The command to come was probably given not to John, but to the first rider.

The first rider appeared to John on a white horse (verse 2). He had a bow in his hand, was given a crown, and rode like a conqueror on a mission. Throughout Revelation white is the symbol of holiness. The bow indicates the ability to slay an enemy. The crown is a picture of victory. In chapter 19 another rider on a white horse is clearly identified as Jesus. In that vision the rider of the white horse is nearing his final victory, but this rider is going out into the earth "bent on conquest" (verse 2). We also notice that in this vision all the horses and horsemen represent influences, not individuals. This rider on the white horse, then, is more likely the influence Jesus wields on this earth, the power of his Word.

From the beginning of the New Testament until the Lord returns, the Word of God will be a sharp, penetrating influence on earth. Revelation already pictured the Word as a double-edged sword coming out of the mouth of Jesus (1:16; 2:12). Because the sword symbolizes war in the next vision (verse 4), the bow may have been chosen here to represent the piercing quality of the Word.

God promises that his Word, like a conqueror bent on conquest, "will accomplish what I desire and achieve the purpose for which I sent it" (Isaiah 55:11). The Word achieves a crown of victory when it wins the hearts of men for the Lamb. In a world of war, famine, and death, the rider on the white horse represents the only hope for conquest. When Jesus prophesied of the last times, he said that his Word would be an ever-present influence throughout the world: "This gospel of the kingdom will be preached in the whole world as a testimony to all nations, and then the end will come" (Matthew 24:14).

The second seal: the red horse

3When the Lamb opened the second seal, I heard the second living creature say, "Come!" 4Then another horse came out, a fiery red one. Its rider was given power to take peace from the earth and to make men slay each other. To him was given a large sword.

The second seal is broken and the second living creature beckons the second horse. John sees a rider on a "fiery, red" horse (verse 4). We find relatively little symbolism in this

picture. Red occurs a number of times in Revelation to symbolize the evil that leads to shedding blood. The sword is an
implement of bloodshed. The large sword is the influence
that greed, anger, and vengeance wield to bring about wars
until the end of history. It steals peace from the earth and
makes men kill each other. There is no doubt that this horse-
man is war. Immediately we recall that Jesus predicted "wars
and rumors of wars. . . . Nation will rise against nation, and
kingdom against kingdom" (Matthew 24:6).

The third seal: the black horse

⁵**When the Lamb opened the third seal, I heard the third living creature say, "Come!" I looked, and there before me was a
black horse! Its rider was holding a pair of scales in his hand.
⁶Then I heard what sounded like a voice among the four living
creatures, saying, "A quart of wheat for a day's wages, and
three quarts of barley for a day's wages, and do not damage
the oil and the wine!"**

After Jesus breaks the third seal, the third living creature
summons the third horse and rider (verse 5). A black horse
comes into sight. Its rider held a pair of scales in his hand.
This was a balance scale to measure bulk food commodities.
A measured weight was put on one side of the scale, and the
food container on the other side was filled until the scale
balanced.

John heard "what sounded like a voice among the four living creatures" (verse 6). It may have been one of the living
creatures, or it may have been more than one voice; John was
not sure. All living creatures on earth depend on food to sus-
tain them. What the voice says displays the anguish God's
living creatures experience when the rider on the black horse
appears with the scales. The price of food is exorbitantly
high: a whole day's pay for a quart of wheat! "Do not dam-

age" may mean, "Do not deal it unjustly." Dishonest sellers might water down oil and wine in order to make more money from it.

The market scales and the prohibitive food prices signal famine. John's language does not allow us to say whether the high prices and the dishonest scales caused the famine or happened because of it. A shortage of food can be brought about by drought or economic inequity, and often, as in the order of the horsemen, famine follows war.

The vision does not reveal the cause of famine, but the color of the horse signifies its results. Black is the color of hopelessness and death. Famines and starvation will occur until the end of the world. Jesus predicted "there will be famines . . . in various places" (Matthew 24:7). Our Lord taught believers to pray for their "daily bread" (Luke 11:3) and told them not to worry about "what [they] will eat" (Matthew 6:25). King David lived a lifetime without seeing God's people suffer from hunger (Psalm 37:25). Yet the sin, war, and natural disaster that cause famine all over the world remind us that "man does not live on bread alone" (Matthew 4:4).

The fourth seal: the pale horse

⁷When the Lamb opened the fourth seal, I heard the voice of the fourth living creature say, "Come!" ⁸I looked, and there before me was a pale horse! Its rider was named Death, and Hades was following close behind him. They were given power over a fourth of the earth to kill by sword, famine and plague, and by the wild beasts of the earth.

When the Lamb opened the fourth seal (verse 7), John heard the fourth living creature summon the fourth horse and rider. The fourth horse is "pale" in color (verse 8). Actually, the Greek word means a pale, sickly green, the color that starvation and disease bring to the human face. The symbolism of this horse is revealed by the name of its rider, "Death" (verse 8).

Following closely behind the pale horse and its rider was "Hades" (verse 8). We must keep from reading too much into this picture. John does not say whether Hades followed on another horse, rode behind Death on the pale horse, or walked along behind him. It doesn't matter. Hades closely follows death. In the New Testament Hades may mean hell or the condition of the dead prior to the final judgment. In Revelation the "second death" (20:14) signifies the condition of the unbeliever that begins at death and continues through the judgment into eternal hell. Here Hades refers to "the silence of death" (Psalm 94:17) before the judgment (see 20:13).

Until Jesus returns, we all live "in the land of the shadow of death" (Isaiah 9:2). "Sword, famine and plague, and . . . wild beasts" (verse 8) are war and crime, starvation and disease, natural disaster and accident. The quarter of the earth's population affected by death in the vision is figurative. It symbolizes the pervasive influence of this pale horse rider at all times in history. Daily news reports drive us to the warning and comfort in our traditional Lutheran funeral rite: "In the midst of life we are in death. Of whom may we seek comfort but of Thee, O Lord?" (*The Pastor's Companion*, Concordia Publishing House, p. 94).

The Lamb opens the fifth seal: the souls under the altar

⁹When he opened the fifth seal, I saw under the altar the souls of those who had been slain because of the word of God and the testimony they had maintained. ¹⁰They called out in a loud voice, "How long, Sovereign Lord, holy and true, until you judge the inhabitants of the earth and avenge our blood?"

79

¹¹Then each of them was given a white robe, and they were told to wait a little longer, until the number of their fellow servants and brothers who were to be killed as they had been was completed.

"The Lamb" (verses 1,3,5,7) opened the first four seals, and the four living creatures called forth the four horsemen and their riders. In line with the symbolism of the number 4, all the events of the first four seals take place on the earth. Beginning with the fifth seal, the scene shifts to things that take place in heaven, to the throne of the triune God (see 5:6). Although it is clear that the Lamb also opens the last three seals of this vision, John refers to him all three times with the pronoun "he" (verses 9,12; 8:1).

The fifth seal reveals the souls of the martyred saints under the altar (verse 9). Judgment day had not arrived, but the souls of those who died for their faith were already in heaven. This coincides with what Jesus told the dying thief: "I tell you the truth, today you will be with me in paradise" (Luke 23:43). The souls of believers go to heaven the instant they pass out of this life. So while Hades sometimes refers to the condition of all who die (see verse 8), it is only speaking about how people on earth consider the dead. Heaven, or paradise, however, is what the souls of believers actually experience until the judgment.

John says he saw the souls of martyrs under "the altar" (verse 9). He is not talking about a particular altar in heaven because Scripture nowhere mentions such an altar. The altar is a part of the symbolism of the sacrifice the martyrs made when they were put to death for what they believed.

The word "slain" (verse 9) means "put to death like a sacrificial animal." This does not imply that the sacrifice of a Christian martyr is a payment for sin. By his sacrificial death,

Jesus "has made perfect forever those who are being made holy. . . . there is no longer any sacrifice for sin" (Hebrews 10:14,18). Rather, like the incense prayers of the saints (see 5:8), a martyr's death is a thank-offering that praises the Lamb for his perfect sacrifice.

The saints under the altar died "because of the word of God and the testimony they had maintained" (verse 9). God's Word always produces more than a quiet conviction in the heart. When the Sanhedrin commanded their silence, Peter and John replied, "We cannot help speaking about what we have seen and heard" (Acts 4:20). Peter's soul was already under the altar when John wrote Revelation—which he wrote from exile on Patmos because of the testimony he had maintained (see 1:9). Many wear the name Christian while hiding behind the safety of silence. Paul, however, wrote, "It is with your heart that you believe and are justified, and it is with your mouth that you confess and are saved" (Romans 10:10).

The souls under the altar wanted to know how long it would be until Jesus returned with final justice and judgment (verse 10). Although in heaven, they were not yet in eternity, so they could sense the passing of time. They did not know the future, and they were not able to see exactly what was happening to those they left behind. Yet they knew that the faithful would continue to suffer persecution and death until the Lamb administered final justice.

Their call for Jesus to "judge" and "avenge" (verse 10) may strike us as unloving. But the martyrs are not praying that their enemies die in unbelief or even that their friends be spared death. Rather, they are asking Jesus for what he already promised, that is, that the last days "be shortened" (Matthew 24:22) for the sake of the elect. Jesus tells them to "wait a little longer" (verse 11). God's loving plans for the

81

future of those he has elected are hidden even from the saints in heaven.

The Lamb opens the sixth seal: the end times

The last judgment

¹²I watched as he opened the sixth seal. There was a great earthquake. The sun turned black like sackcloth made of goat hair, the whole moon turned blood red, ¹³and the stars in the sky fell to earth, as late figs drop from a fig tree when shaken by a strong wind. ¹⁴The sky receded like a scroll, rolling up, and every mountain and island was removed from its place.

¹⁵Then the kings of the earth, the princes, the generals, the rich, the mighty, and every slave and every free man hid in caves and among the rocks of the mountains. ¹⁶They called to the mountains and the rocks, "Fall on us and hide us from the face of him who sits on the throne and from the wrath of the Lamb! ¹⁷For the great day of their wrath has come, and who can stand?"

The seven seals of the second vision put into pictures what Jesus prophesied in Matthew 24. The first four seals depict the four major influences on earth throughout history. The last three seals picture the activity that takes place in heaven just before the end of the world. Verses 12 through 17 relate what is happening on earth as a backdrop to chapter 7, which records the activity in heaven during this end time.

John watched the Lamb open the sixth seal. We cannot explain all the fantastic images of natural disaster he sees (verses 12-14). John's words correspond to the prophecies of Isaiah (Isaiah 13:10; 34:4) and Jesus (Matthew 24:29). The symbolism does not say the earth will be annihilated. John is describing the destructive changes to this sin-spoiled world that will prepare for "a new heaven and a new earth" (21:1).

The rich descriptions he used here are later summarized in a single verse: "The first earth had passed away" (21:1).

John's attention is turned from the dramatic disturbances in nature to what is going on among the people on earth (verse 15). From verse 16 we can see that all six of the classes of people he mentions are unbelievers. The way John phrases "every slave and every free man" (verse 15) shows that he includes "every slave" and "every free man" in one class of people. The six classes symbolize the total of evil men on earth.

Those who despised the Lamb search in vain for protection among the natural formations of the earth. Their futile cry to be protected from the coming wrath was prophesied by Hosea (Hosea 10:8) and Jesus (Luke 23:30). The rest of Revelation speaks only of the wrath of God, but here it is the wrath of the Lamb (verse 16). God is the Lamb they pierced and now must face in the judgment (1:7).

The 144,000 on earth

7 After this I saw four angels standing at the four corners of the earth, holding back the four winds of the earth to prevent any wind from blowing on the land or on the sea or on any tree. ²Then I saw another angel coming up from the east, having the seal of the living God. He called out in a loud voice to the four angels who had been given power to harm the land and the sea: ³"Do not harm the land or the sea or the trees until we put a seal on the foreheads of the servants of our God." ⁴Then I heard the number of those who were sealed: 144,000 from all the tribes of Israel.

⁵ From the tribe of Judah 12,000 were sealed,
   from the tribe of Reuben 12,000,
   from the tribe of Gad 12,000,
⁶ from the tribe of Asher 12,000,

from the tribe of Naphtali 12,000,
from the tribe of Manasseh 12,000,
⁷ from the tribe of Simeon 12,000,
from the tribe of Levi 12,000,
from the tribe of Issachar 12,000,
⁸ from the tribe of Zebulun 12,000,
from the tribe of Joseph 12,000,
from the tribe of Benjamin 12,000.

John writes many lines of beautiful imagery to detail all that happens in an instant on judgment day. Jesus prophesied, "For as lightning that comes from the east is visible even in the west, so will be the coming of the Son of Man" (Matthew 24:27). Paul, speaking literally, wrote that all these things will happen "in a flash, in the twinkling of an eye, at the last trumpet" (1 Corinthians 15:52). What we must understand about John's imagery, then, is that all he sees from chapter 6:12 to the end of chapter 7 happens in the blink of an eye.

When John says, "After this" (verse 1), he is talking about time that passed for him, not time that elapsed since the events of the preceding verses (see 4:1). This activity of the four angels on behalf of believers corresponds to the day of judgment for unbelievers. Verses 1 to 8 describe the work of the angels in gathering the elect to heaven before the destruction of the earth and the unbelievers. Jesus said this "harvest is the end of the age, and the harvesters are angels. This is how it will be at the end of the age. The angels will come and separate the wicked from the righteous" (Matthew 13:39,49).

Again, we must take this whole section as a unit, so we interpret its symbolism in a way that agrees with Jesus' literal words of prophecy. The angels God sends to gather believers to himself in heaven must not allow the destruction of the earth until the faithful are marked as his and taken to heaven. The winds picture the destructive forces that will bring an end

to the world as we know it. That is why God sends another
angel (verse 2) to restrain the four angels with the winds: "Do
not harm the land or the sea or the trees until we put a seal on
the foreheads of the servants of our God" (verse 3).

A seal is a mark of personal identification. The seals on
the scroll (5:1) were made of wax impressed with a metal
die. The seals on the foreheads of believers were more likely
made with permanent ink, or dye. Marking the believers with
a seal does not signify God's work of preserving them in
faith throughout their earthly life, but his public recognition
of them at the final judgment. From the moment of faith,
believers are "a people belonging to God" (1 Peter 2:9).
While we are on earth, our "life is . . . hidden with Christ in
God. When Christ, who is [our] life, appears, then [we] also
will appear with him in glory" (Colossians 3:3,4).

Verses 4 through 8 offer a symbolic picture of all those
God elected to salvation and preserved in faith. Although the
12 tribes of Israel are used to communicate this picture, it is
clear that not only Old Testament believers are to be understood by it. The 12 tribes are listed in this order nowhere else
in Scripture, which reinforces the symbolic nature of this picture. The New Testament talks about a spiritual Israel that
includes all believers (see 2:9). In this sense Paul writes, "So
all Israel will be saved" (Romans 11:26). Verse 9 removes
any question that these are all the elect when it says they
come from "every nation, tribe, people and language."

Since 12 is the product of 3, the number for God, and 4,
the number for humanity, the number 12 and its multiples
signify the completion of God's covenant of grace with all
people. In any case, the next verse proves the number
144,000 to be purely symbolic. These same elect are
described as "a great multitude that no one could count"
(verse 9).

85

The great white host in heaven

⁹After this I looked and there before me was a great multitude that no one could count, from every nation, tribe, people and language, standing before the throne and in front of the Lamb. They were wearing white robes and were holding palm branches in their hands. ¹⁰And they cried out in a loud voice:

"Salvation belongs to our God,
who sits on the throne,
and to the Lamb."

¹¹All the angels were standing around the throne and around the elders and the four living creatures. They fell down on their faces before the throne and worshiped God, ¹²saying:

"Amen!
Praise and glory and wisdom and thanks and honor
and power and strength
be to our God for ever and ever.
Amen!"

¹³Then one of the elders asked me, "These in white robes—who are they, and where did they come from?"

¹⁴I answered, "Sir, you know."

And he said, "These are they who have come out of the great tribulation; they have washed their robes and made them white in the blood of the Lamb. ¹⁵Therefore,

"they are before the throne of God
and serve him day and night in his temple;
and he who sits on the throne will spread his tent
over them.
¹⁶ Never again will they hunger;
never again will they thirst.
The sun will not beat upon them,
nor any scorching heat.
¹⁷ For the Lamb at the center of the throne
will be their shepherd;

he will lead them to springs of living water.
And God will wipe away every tear from their eyes."

John again writes, "After this I looked" (verse 9). Time passes for John as he watches one scene follow another in the sixth seal of the scroll. But the passage of time from the events of one scene to the next is not as great as it is for John to watch them. The three scenes of the sixth seal first picture the unbelievers on earth (6:12-17), then the elect on earth (7:1-8), and now the elect in heaven (7:9-17). On the great and glorious day of Jesus' return, all these things will happen within a very brief time. — P. 84 SAYS INSTANT

Paul's description of judgment day provides details of what will happen between the time the angels seal the elect on earth and the time the elect stand before the throne in heaven: "The Lord himself will come down from heaven, with a loud command, with the voice of the archangel and with the trumpet call of God, and the dead in Christ will rise first. After that, we who are still alive and are left will be caught up together with them in the clouds to meet the Lord in the air. And so we will be with the Lord forever" (1 Thessalonians 4:16,17).

John sees a multitude too large to count before the throne. This multitude includes all whom God elected to salvation: the believers of the Old Testament, the saints and martyrs of the New Testament, and the elect who were still alive on earth when the last trumpet call was sounded. The four word description "nation, tribe, people and language" symbolically indicates all the elect from the earth. The multitude of believers that stands "before the throne and in front of the Lamb" (verse 9) strikes a sharp contrast to those who tried to hide "from the face of him who sits on the throne and from the wrath of the Lamb" (6:16).

The white robes they wore signify the righteousness Jesus credited to them when he washed away their sins in his blood (see 3:4,5 and verses 13,14 below). The palm branches they held showed that they were ready to participate in the festive praise of the victors. Their joyful cry is "Salvation belongs to our God" (verse 10), that is, God is to be credited with our salvation. The God who sits on the throne is mentioned in the same breath as the Lamb who stands "in the center of the throne" (5:6).

The angels, the elders, and the four living creatures add their praise to the worship of the saints. When we hear this, we must remember that we are dealing with highly symbolic language. The 24 elders represent all believers. The four living creatures stand for all the living creatures on earth, including all people. To see the elders and the living creatures join the saints seems redundant. When reading the apocalypse's rich symbolism, however, we must look at the whole picture and not press the details. The whole picture describes an awesome gathering of millions of voices of the faithful from earth and heaven. The main object of their attention is the One on the throne and the Lamb. Ours must be too.

First, this new group of worshipers says, "Amen" (verse 12) to the praise the saints have raised to God. Then they ascribe seven different words of praise to the eternal God. Earlier, both the four living creatures (see 4:8) and the elders (see 4:11) offered three-part verses of praise. Now God, represented by the number 3, has completed his covenant of grace with the elect from the earth, represented by the number 4 (see verse 9), and the elders and the living creatures join in a seven-part verse of praise.

The believers are praising God for all the things that he has performed to bring them salvation. Praise never gives God anything. "Who has ever given to God . . . ?" (Romans

11:35). When the believers say praise "be to our God," they were acknowledging that these things already belonged to him. Again the angels, elders, and living creatures say, "Amen," that is, "This is certainly true."

Verses 13 through 17 reveal where the white-robed multitude came from and where they are now. They have "come out of the great tribulation" (verse 14) and are now "before the throne of God" (verse 15). The subject of the conversation between the elder and John is how this great escape and present glory were made possible. The answer lies in the white robes that the multitude was wearing (see verse 8).

The white robes have appeared before. To Sardis Jesus promised, "He who overcomes will, like them, be dressed in white" (3:5). The 24 elders, representative of all believers, "were dressed in white" (4:4) too. Now the symbolism of the white robes is explained: "They have washed their robes and made them white in the blood of the Lamb" (verse 14). Forgiveness is a single loving action that the Bible describes in two ways. In the same instant that God cleanses our filthy rags, he credits Jesus' perfection to us as a white robe of righteousness. This truth is well expressed in the following hymn stanza: "Jesus, your blood and righteousness my beauty are, my glorious dress; Mid flaming worlds, in these arrayed, with joy shall I lift up my head" (CW 376:1).

The events of judgment day all happen in a moment. In verse 14 the white-robed saints enter heaven. This takes place within the same brief time as the events at the end of chapter 6 and the beginning of chapter 7. Although the NIV translation says, "These are they who have come out of the great tribulation" (verse 14), John actually used a present tense verb. He described the multitude in white as those who *are coming* out of the great tribulation. While unbelievers stand in fear, the elect are gathered and enter heaven.

John's use of the present tense here contradicts the mil-lennialistic notion that God will rapture some believers from the earth to spare them the tribulation. Judgment day, not a rapture, will deliver the justice for God's suffering people for which the martyrs asked (see 6:10). God does not promise here or anywhere that he will spare believers the anguish of the last days. Rather, Jesus warned, "In this world you will have trouble" (John 16:33). Paul and Barn-abas encouraged the early Christians to "remain true to the faith" not with the promise of a rapture, but with this reminder: "We must go through many hardships to enter the kingdom of God" (Acts 14:22).

Revelation provides many wonderful glimpses of heaven. None is more beautiful than the description of the saints in verses 15 to 17. Appropriately, the bliss of heaven is first defined by the presence of the saints "before the throne of God" (verse 15). God and the Lamb are the reason the saints are in heaven. David looked forward to this bliss when he wrote, "You will fill me with joy in your presence, with eter-nal pleasures at your right hand" (Psalm 16:11). Those who imagine heaven as a boring place with nothing to do but play harps are wrong. Believers will find fulfilling service day and night.

God's presence protects the saints from every evil power. The tent of God's protection will shield us from every sorrow that sin and Satan cause us on earth. The vision portrays the perfect unity of the Father and the Son as "he who sits on the throne" and "the Lamb at the center of the throne" (verses 15,17; see 5:1,6). The Good Shepherd who pastured his sheep on earth beside the "quiet waters" of his Word (Psalm 23:2), will now "lead them to springs of living water" (verse 17). Living water means "eternal life" (John 4:10,13,14).

VISION OF THE TRUMPETS
(8:1–11:19)

The Lamb opens the seventh seal: the vision of the trumpets

Seven angels with seven trumpets

8 When he opened the seventh seal, there was silence in heaven for about half an hour.

²And I saw the seven angels who stand before God, and to them were given seven trumpets.

³Another angel, who had a golden censer, came and stood at the altar. He was given much incense to offer, with the prayers of all the saints, on the golden altar before the throne. ⁴The smoke of the incense, together with the prayers of the saints, went up before God from the angel's hand. ⁵Then the angel took the censer, filled it with fire from the altar, and hurled it on the earth; and there came peals of thunder, rumblings, flashes of lightning and an earthquake.

As the second vision ends, it folds into the third. The seventh seal of the vision of the scroll introduces the third vision, the vision of the seven trumpets. The blending of the second vision into the third shows a close relationship between the events in both. The first four seals of the second vision unfolded events in the physical world. The last three seals pictured the spiritual world's influence on the inhabitants of the earth. The vision of the trumpets follows the same division into four and three. The first four trumpets announce events on earth in a relatively few verses (8:6-12). Then the last three trumpets announce the influence of the spirit world on the earth with great detail (8:13-11:19).

Only the Lamb was worthy to open the seven seals of the scroll that unfolds the future. John mentioned the Lamb by name at the opening of the first four seals but refers to him only with the pronoun *he* when the last three are opened (see 6:9). After the Lamb opened the seventh seal, there was a pause in heaven to draw attention to the importance of what was coming (verse 1).

During this silence "the seven angels" (verse 2) before God are given seven trumpets. Besides this verse, the Bible nowhere speaks of seven particular angels in the presence of God. There is probably more significance in the angels' number than in their identity. The number 7 is the sum of 3, the number of God, and 4, the number of earth or humanity. The seven angels, then, may symbolize the agents God uses to warn the people of the earth about the future revealed in the next seven scenes. Trumpets were used on battlefields and in temples and palaces to call attention to pronouncements.

Another angel enters John's view. This might be an archangel like the one who came to seal the elect (7:2). This angel may also represent Jesus. The Scriptures often speak of the Son of God as an angel, especially in the first six books of the Old Testament, where he is called the Angel of the Lord. The angel's activity in verses 3 through 5 also suggests this angel is Jesus.

The angel carried a golden censer to the altar. The mention of this altar, as well as other altars and incense in Revelation, seems to draw from the arrangement of the Old Testament tabernacle. The temple included an altar of incense overlaid with gold (Exodus 30:1-5). In an earlier scene (5:8), incense was the prayers of the saints, but here the incense is added to the prayers of the saints. Because we sinners cannot approach God on our own merit, the incense may represent the Lamb's intercession on our behalf. Or if we consider this angel to be an archangel, the incense may signify what the Holy Spirit adds to our prayers. "We do not know what we ought to pray for, but the Spirit himself intercedes for us with groans that words cannot express" (Romans 8:26).

"The angel took the censer, filled it with fire from the altar, and hurled it on the earth" (verse 5). The angel's actions are precipitated by the mix of incense and the prayers of the saints. John was writing to a persecuted church looking for God's final justice. The prayers of the saints on earth no doubt echoed the plea of the martyrs under the altar, "How long?" (6:10). The fire from the altar is the "wrath of the Lamb" (6:16). When the angel hurls the censer to earth, he signals that events leading to final justice for the saints are being set in motion. All of nature reacts violently to the announcement.

Four angels sound their trumpets

⁶Then the seven angels who had the seven trumpets prepared to sound them.

⁷The first angel sounded his trumpet, and there came hail and fire mixed with blood, and it was hurled down upon the earth. A third of the earth was burned up, a third of the trees were burned up, and all the green grass was burned up.

⁸The second angel sounded his trumpet, and something like a huge mountain, all ablaze, was thrown into the sea. A third of the sea turned into blood, ⁹a third of the living creatures in the sea died, and a third of the ships were destroyed.

¹⁰The third angel sounded his trumpet, and a great star, blazing like a torch, fell from the sky on a third of the rivers and on the springs of water—¹¹the name of the star is Wormwood. A third of the waters turned bitter, and many people died from the waters that had become bitter.

¹²The fourth angel sounded his trumpet, and a third of the sun was struck, a third of the moon, and a third of the stars, so

that a third of them turned dark. A third of the day was without light, and also a third of the night.

Now the seven angels with the seven trumpets, introduced in verse 2, step forward (verse 6). The first four angels trumpet natural disasters. Although the language in verses 7 to 13 is vivid, the meaning is not clear. John does not explain these pictures or stop to interpret details, as he sometimes does in other visions. For this reason, people have assigned many different meanings to these four trumpets.

Two things help us gain at least a little understanding of these verses. First, the folding of the last seal of the scroll into this vision of the trumpets suggests a parallel between the two visions.

Since the first four seals of the second vision were all events that took place on earth before the judgment, it is likely that these four trumpets describe the same arena and time period. Then, if we view all four trumpets as a single picture, without forcing meaning on every detail, we see that this whole section describes natural disasters on earth.

The first four trumpets of the seven angels, then, are God's warning to the church that the degeneration of the natural world signals its final destruction on judgment day. This thought aligns with what Scripture teaches. "We know that the whole creation has been groaning as in the pains of childbirth right up to the present time" (Romans 8:22). It is not hard to see how sin has taken its toll in the created world with forest fires, pollution of waterways, the destruction of wildlife, and sun-darkening smog. The rate of natural destruction and the appearance of great natural disasters will accelerate as the end nears. Jesus said, "There will be signs in the sun, moon and stars . . . roaring and tossing of the sea. . . . heavenly bodies will be shaken" (Luke 21:25,26). Every

94

generation has seen the warning of these four trumpets fulfilled to some degree. Our Lord's words pertain to every generation: "When you see all these things, you know that it is
near, right at the door" (Matthew 24:33).

Three angels sound the last trumpets

The fifth trumpet: the first woe

[13]As I watched, I heard an eagle that was flying in midair
call out in a loud voice: "Woe! Woe! Woe to the inhabitants of
the earth, because of the trumpet blasts about to be sounded
by the other three angels!"

9 The fifth angel sounded his trumpet, and I saw a star that
had fallen from the sky to the earth. The star was given the
key to the shaft of the Abyss. [2]When he opened the Abyss,
smoke rose from it like the smoke from a gigantic furnace. The
sun and sky were darkened by the smoke from the Abyss. [3]And
out of the smoke locusts came down upon the earth and were
given power like that of scorpions of the earth. [4]They were told
not to harm the grass of the earth or any plant or tree, but only
those people who did not have the seal of God on their foreheads. [5]They were not given power to kill them, but only to torture them for five months. And the agony they suffered was
like that of the sting of a scorpion when it strikes a man. [6]Dur-
ing those days men will seek death, but will not find it; they
will long to die, but death will elude them.

[7]The locusts looked like horses prepared for battle. On their
heads they wore something like crowns of gold, and their faces
resembled human faces. [8]Their hair was like women's hair, and
their teeth were like lions' teeth. [9]They had breastplates like
breastplates of iron, and the sound of their wings was like the
thundering of many horses and chariots rushing into battle.
[10]They had tails and stings like scorpions, and in their tails they
had power to torment people for five months. [11]They had as
king over them the angel of the Abyss, whose name in Hebrew
is Abaddon, and in Greek, Apollyon.

After the first four trumpets, John heard "an eagle" make a dire announcement (8:13). The loud voice of the eagle provides a transition from the first four trumpets to the last three. The eagle brings a warning from the triune God, so he repeats three times, "Woe! Woe! Woe . . ." The symbolic 3 reminds us that God allows and limits the evil that afflicts the earth. The incense burner that was hurled to earth (8:5) is a sign that God's judgment is responding to the wrath of the Lamb and the prayers of the saints.

The fifth angel trumpets the first woe. John saw a star fall from the sky (verse 1). Stars appear in Revelation both as a part of the natural world and as symbols of leaders. In the seven letters to the churches, the stars referred to the spiritual leaders of the congregations. Here the star refers to an evil spiritual leader, the devil. The star that "was given the key to the shaft of the Abyss" (verse 1) is the same as "the angel of the Abyss" mentioned in verse 11.

An abyss is a bottomless pit. This is a specific abyss, the "darkness" of hell, where Satan is kept "bound with everlasting chains for judgment on the great Day" (Jude 6). Notice that John did not see the star fall from the sky. This star "had fallen" earlier (verse 1). Long ago God had expelled Satan from heaven. The key that God gives Satan symbolizes that the devil does not have free rein on the earth. For example, Satan had to ask God for permission to test Job, and he does not have the power to release the evil angels on earth except by God's allowance.

The picture here is a little different but sends the same message as chapter 20, verse 3. As we near judgment day, Satan will "be set free for a short time" (20:3). When Satan unlocked the Abyss (verse 2), smoke billowed out and darkened the sun. Jesus spoke of "the fire of hell" (Matthew

5:22). The darkening of the sun pictures the influence of those released from "the darkness" (Matthew 8:12).

From the opening symbolism of this woe, we gain the ability to interpret some of the more difficult language that follows. The locusts that appeared out of the smoke (verse 3) are Satan's helpers, the evil angels. Again, we note that they were given power. God authorized their limited activity.

But God placed four restrictions on them. First, they were not to harm the natural world. This means that the damage described in this woe, unlike that of the first four trumpets, is spiritual in nature. The locust demons went out into the world to tempt men and promote false teachings. But God also limits the spiritual damage they can do. They could only inflict their evil on those "who did not have the seal of God on their foreheads" (verse 4).

The seal of God symbolizes God's elect (7:3). Jesus made a promise about them: "No one can snatch them out of my Father's hand" (John 10:29). Even the devils' effect on unbelievers is limited. They may not kill anyone. That power God reserves for himself. "I put to death and I bring to life" he says (Deuteronomy 32:39). Finally, God limits the time they can wreak their spiritual havoc to "five months" (verse 5). The number 10 stands for a specific limit that God sets (see 2:10). The number 5, half of 10, doubly emphasizes the limited duration John later describes as a "short time" (20:3).

In spite of these four limitations, the impact of the demons on earth will be painful. Three times John mentions the scorpion-like nature of the locusts (verses 3,5,10). The devils' sting stands for the painful consequences of temptation and false doctrine. Already before death, sin exacts its wages. These include a guilty conscience, bitter remorse, and the painful consequences of an immoral lifestyle. The vision does not identify the sting of the scorpion; it only pictures a pain so severe that those afflicted by it want to die.

Verses 7 to 10 paint many stunning details into one picture. It is not as important to interpret each of the details as it is to notice the theme of the painting. The devils' temptations and false teachings wear many faces. Some of these faces are aggressive and powerful, like the horses, chariots, and tails (verses 7,9,10). Some are deceptively attractive— notice the crowns, human faces, and women's hair (verses 7,8). These are not real crowns but something like crowns. Satan and his allies can pose as saints—who wear the real crowns (2:10; 3:11)—when they tempt and mislead. The sharp teeth and stings are another reminder of the pain sin causes.

The star that fell from heaven and loosed this plague of evil locusts on the earth is now identified (verse 11). He is the evil angel of hell. The names John calls him occur only here in the Bible, so John explains them. They are the Hebrew and Greek names for *Destroyer*. These are appropriate names for the devil. His more common name, Satan, means "the accuser." Satan's accusations first lead men to despair and then to destruction.

A warning is given here to all who are complacent about their faith. "Our struggle is not against flesh and blood, but against the rulers, against the authorities, against the powers of this dark world and against the spiritual forces of evil in the heavenly realms" (Ephesians 6:12). To encourage us in our lifelong struggle against the king of the Abyss, Paul writes, "Put on the full armor of God so that you can take your stand against the devil's schemes" (Ephesians 6:11).

The sixth trumpet: the second woe

Army of the four angels

[12]The first woe is past; two other woes are yet to come.

[13]The sixth angel sounded his trumpet, and I heard a voice coming from the horns of the golden altar that is before God. [14]It said to the sixth angel who had the trumpet, "Release the four angels who are bound at the great river Euphrates." [15]And the four angels who had been kept ready for this very hour and day and month and year were released to kill a third of mankind. [16]The number of the mounted troops was two hundred million. I heard their number.

[17]The horses and riders I saw in my vision looked like this: Their breastplates were fiery red, dark blue, and yellow as sulfur. The heads of the horses resembled the heads of lions, and out of their mouths came fire, smoke and sulfur. [18]A third of mankind was killed by the three plagues of fire, smoke and sulfur that came out of their mouths. [19]The power of the horses was in their mouths and in their tails; for their tails were like snakes, having heads with which they inflict injury.

[20]The rest of mankind that were not killed by these plagues still did not repent of the work of their hands; they did not stop worshiping demons, and idols of gold, silver, bronze, stone and wood—idols that cannot see or hear or walk. [21]Nor did they repent of their murders, their magic arts, their sexual immorality or their thefts.

"The first woe is past; two other woes are yet to come" (verse 12). The eagle who announced the three "Woes" (8:13) may have spoken these words. After his loud voice announced the three "Woes," the fifth angel had trumpeted the first woe (9:1). Now, when he announces that other woes are yet to come, the sixth angel sounds the trumpet for the second woe (verse 13).

"The number of the mounted troops was two hundred million. I heard their number." (9:16)

John heard a voice coming from the altar in heaven. The horns recall details of the altar in the Old Testament. Since God had promised his presence there, the voice John hears is the voice of God. That becomes certain when the voice commands the release of the four angels at the Euphrates river. In the first woe we learned that only God can restrict the activity of evil angels. That truth is reinforced here.

These four angels are not the same as the four angels in chapter 7, verse 1. Those were good angels who sealed God's elect. These are evil angels who carry out evil and had to be "bound" (verse 14). This woe again points out that God allows evil to serve his good purpose. God not only controls the amount of evil and its duration (see 9:4,5), but he also dictates the "very hour and day and month and year" it can begin (verse 15). In the middle of the picture of woe are clear indications of God's love for the saints.

The number 4 suggests that these evil angels will afflict the earth. They were bound at the Euphrates river, which runs through the cradle of civilization. The great ancient kingdoms of this region carried God's Old Testament people into captivity. The four angels, then, originate from the demonic source of opposition to God's people.

On this mission of evil, however, God restricts their activity to bringing judgment on unbelievers. Their mission is "to kill a third of mankind" (verse 15). God utters no specific instruction not to harm believers, as he did in the first woe (see 9:4). But it is clear from verse 20 that *mankind* refers not to all people, but to the unrepentant.

The description of the horde of troops in verses 16 to 19 is best viewed as one picture. The picture as a whole depicts the devastating influence of evil angels on the unrepentant. "Two hundred million" (verse 16) indicates that devils are innumerable. Although John sees "mounted troops" (verse 16), the horses cause the damage. Yet the colors of the riders' breastplates correspond to the colors of hell (see 9:2) that came out of the horses' mouths. This may indicate the cooperative attack of evil angels and their human representatives to tempt people and teach false doctrine.

Many similarities exist between this woe and the first one. Both show us how God allows evil forces to afflict unbelievers. Both graphically portray the power and deceit of temptation and false teaching, as well as their devastating results.

There seems to be some progression of time, however, from the first woe to the second. In the first woe the demon locusts were not allowed to kill anyone, but in this woe a third of the unbelieving world, that is, a very large number of unbelievers, will be killed. As the end nears God will allow the consequences of sin and false doctrine to take their toll more dramatically.

Yet notice the holy frustration of a patient God who predicts that they "still did not repent" (verse 20). Whenever God allows evil, even the kind of horrible destruction pictured here, he has a loving purpose. He is giving the unrepentant one more opportunity to see the consequences of their sin and turn from it. Peter wrote of this loving purpose of God without symbolic language: "The Lord is not slow in keeping his promise, as some understand slowness. He is patient with you, not wanting anyone to perish, but everyone to come to repentance" (2 Peter 3:9).

The list of sins in verse 21 confirms that temptation and false teaching are the destructive forces symbolized by the mounted troops. Demon worship, idolatry, and magic arts are the product of false doctrine. Murder, sexual immorality, and theft are gross sins produced by temptation. More and more, these things will characterize the unbelieving world until the end comes. Little by little, God's patience will run out, and he will allow the terrible consequences of their sins to come on the unrepentant. Still, these are his last loving attempts to draw them to the Lamb.

The angel with the small scroll

10 Then I saw another mighty angel coming down from heaven. He was robed in a cloud, with a rainbow above his head; his face was like the sun, and his legs were like fiery pillars. ²He was holding a little scroll, which lay open in his hand. He planted his right foot on the sea and his left foot on the land, ³and he gave a loud shout like the roar of a lion. When he shouted, the voices of the seven thunders spoke. ⁴And when the seven thunders spoke, I was about to write; but I heard a voice from heaven say, "Seal up what the seven thunders have said and do not write it down."

⁵Then the angel I had seen standing on the sea and on the land raised his right hand to heaven. ⁶And he swore by him who lives for ever and ever, who created the heavens and all that is in them, the earth and all that is in it, and the sea and all that is in it, and said, "There will be no more delay! ⁷But in the days when the seventh angel is about to sound his trumpet, the mystery of God will be accomplished, just as he announced to his servants the prophets."

⁸Then the voice that I had heard from heaven spoke to me once more: "Go, take the scroll that lies open in the hand of the angel who is standing on the sea and on the land."

⁹So I went to the angel and asked him to give me the little scroll. He said to me, "Take it and eat it. It will turn your stomach sour, but in your mouth it will be as sweet as honey." ¹⁰I took the little scroll from the angel's hand and ate it. It tasted as sweet as honey in my mouth, but when I had eaten it, my stomach turned sour. ¹¹Then I was told, "You must prophesy again about many people, nations, languages and kings."

If the angel with the golden censer in chapter 8, verse 3, could be identified as Jesus, it is even more probable that the "mighty angel coming down from heaven" in chapter 10, verse 1, is Jesus too. The description John provides of this angel seems to rule out a created angel or archangel. "He was robed in a cloud" (verse 1). The disciples were surrounded by a cloud at Jesus' transfiguration (Luke 9:34), and Jesus said that he would return "in a cloud with power and great glory" (Luke 21:27; see 1:7). The Bible never speaks of a created angel clothed in a cloud.

The other descriptions also point to Jesus. He has a rainbow over his head. In chapter 4, verse 3, a rainbow encircles the throne of God and in chapter 5, verse 6, the Lamb is "standing in the center of the throne." The angel's face shone like the sun, just as Jesus' did at his transfiguration (Matthew 17:2) and as John has already described in chapter 1, verse 16. The legs "like fiery pillars" (verse 1) resemble the feet like bronze glowing in a furnace in chapter 1, verse 15.

In the hand of this angel was "a little scroll" (verse 2). Unlike the scroll of chapter 5 with seven seals, this scroll was open. It had been opened some time in the past and was still lying open. The open-book nature of this scroll is a clue to its contents, which will be revealed at the end of this chapter.

With one foot on the land and the other on the sea, the angel is poised to make an announcement to the whole world. His lion-like shout cues the voices of the seven thunders. John heard what the thunders said but was instructed not to write it down (verse 4). Thunder often accompanies God's wrath (Isaiah 29:6). The voices may have described how God would carry out his judgment against the unrepentant, but the voice from heaven did not want us to have those details.

We may not know exactly how God will carry out his anger against the unrepentant in the last days, yet suffering Christians may know with certainty that the time when God will bring final justice is not far off. The angel, Jesus, swears by the eternal Creator, "There will be no more delay!" (verse 6). Time will run out for those who put off repentance.

The oath that this mighty angel takes sounds like a threat to the unbeliever, but it has the sweet sound of promise to the faithful. The seventh angel John mentions in verse 7 is the angel who will blow what Paul calls "the last trumpet" (1 Corinthians 15:52). When that last trumpet sounds, God will make clear how he will bring justice to his saints and judgment on sinners. What sounds like the foreboding rumbling of thunder to unbelievers signals the accomplishment of God's mystery for the elect.

"The mystery of God" (verse 7) is the gospel in its fullest sense. It includes the message of the Savior promised by the Old Testament prophets. The gospel is a mystery in the sense that it remains enigmatic to the worldly, "for the message of the cross is foolishness to those who are perishing" (1 Corinthians 1:18).

Since Christ's work is completed, however, the mystery that "will be accomplished" (verse 7) must have a broader meaning. It includes gospel promises to the believer that are as yet unfulfilled. "'No mind has conceived what God has prepared for those who love him'—but God has revealed it to us by his Spirit" (1 Corinthians 2:9,10). To the extent that Scripture reveals our future glory, we understand this mystery. But much of the gospel's promise remains unknown even to the faithful. "Your life is now hidden with Christ in God. When Christ, who is your life, appears, then you also will appear with him in glory" (Colossians 3:3,4). When the last trumpet sounds and Christ appears, all the mystery of his gospel promises will disappear in the reality of final glory.

Although the voice from heaven (verse 4) told John not to record the doomsday details of the seven thunders, the same voice instructs him to take the open scroll from the hand of the angel (verse 8). The voice from heaven is the voice of God. His instructions to John in this chapter set the tone for all who read and interpret Revelation. We should not strain to figure out all the details of God's judgment on the unrepentant in the last days. Instead, our task is to take the open book from Jesus' hand and share its contents with the world.

The words of verses 9 to 11 are only mildly figurative. They provide an easy-to-understand outline of believers' activities during the last days. First, we are to eat the little scroll. Then we live with the often bitter consequences. Finally, we make it our life's work to reveal the contents of this open book to the rest of the world.

The angel, whom we have identified as Jesus, gave John the little scroll and told him to eat it. *Eating* often describes the receiving action of faith. Jesus cited Deuteronomy 8:3 to the devil: "Man does not live on bread alone, but on every word that comes from the mouth of God" (Matthew 4:4). One of our old Lutheran liturgical prayers speaks of "inwardly digesting" the Word of God. The angel's instructions to John here closely parallel God's call to Ezekiel to be his prophet (Ezekiel 2:9–3:3,14). Ezekiel also ate the scroll that tasted sweet at first but later became bitter. Ezekiel, like John, was commissioned to share the contents of the scroll with others.

The mystery of the gospel always tastes sweet to those who receive it by faith. The psalmist said that God's words are "sweeter than honey, than honey from the comb" (Psalm 19:10). Since "faith comes from hearing the message"

(Romans 10:17), "eating" the word of Christ is a daily activity in the life of the believer. Jesus said that "those who hear the word of God and obey it" are blessed (Luke 11:28).

But the message that is so sweet to the taste quickly turns sour in the stomach. When we try to digest the truth of the gospel, that is, put it into practice in a wicked world, we experience bitterness. We learn that what is honey to our taste is "a stumbling block to Jews and foolishness to Gentiles" (1 Corinthians 1:23). What Jesus describes figuratively for John as turning sour in the stomach (verse 9), he predicted literally for those living in the last days: "You will be hated by all nations because of me" (Matthew 24:9). Ezekiel also records that he set out to share the contents of the scroll "in bitterness and in the anger of [his] spirit" (Ezekiel 3:14).

Our bittersweet experience with the gospel accompanies us as we set out on our life's mission. We live to bring the contents of the little scroll to the world. We go, trusting that the sweet promises of the gospel will put an end to the uneasiness in our soul. We understand that a part of the mystery of God's grace is that his gospel is meant for all to hear. "This mystery is that through the gospel the Gentiles are heirs together with Israel, members together of one body, and sharers together in the promise in Christ Jesus" (Ephesians 3:6). Believers are happy to suffer the bitterness in order that others may taste the sweet gospel.

This is why Jesus tells John to "prophesy again about many peoples, nations, languages and kings" (verse 11). The fourfold description of the earth's inhabitants emphasizes the universal human audience of the gospel. Jesus' command to prophesy "about" many peoples is better understood as a commission to prophesy to them, or on their behalf. The peoples of the world are not the subjects of the gospel, but the intended audience.

Jesus' words to John in verses 9 to 11 are also his words to us: Grow daily in faith as you hear and read the Word of the gospel. Wrestle with the bitterness of soul that is brought on by living the gospel in an unbelieving world. Make that same sinful world that was the object of my redeeming work your audience for sharing the contents of the scroll.

The two witnesses

11 I was given a reed like a measuring rod and was told, "Go and measure the temple of God and the altar, and count the worshipers there. ²But exclude the outer court; do not measure it, because it has been given to the Gentiles. They will trample on the holy city for 42 months. ³And I will give power to my two witnesses, and they will prophesy for 1,260 days, clothed in sackcloth." ⁴These are the two olive trees and the two lampstands that stand before the Lord of the earth. ⁵If anyone tries to harm them, fire comes from their mouths and devours their enemies. This is how anyone who wants to harm them must die. ⁶These men have power to shut up the sky so that it will not rain during the time they are prophesying; and they have power to turn the waters into blood and to strike the earth with every kind of plague as often as they want.**

⁷Now when they have finished their testimony, the beast that comes up from the Abyss will attack them, and overpower and kill them. ⁸Their bodies will lie in the street of the great city, which is figuratively called Sodom and Egypt, where also their Lord was crucified. ⁹For three and a half days men from every people, tribe, language and nation will gaze on their bodies and refuse them burial. ¹⁰The inhabitants of the earth will gloat over them and will celebrate by sending each other gifts, because these two prophets had tormented those who live on the earth.

¹¹But after three and a half days a breath of life from God entered them, and they stood on their feet, and terror struck those who saw them. ¹²Then they heard a loud voice from

heaven saying to them, "Come up here." And they went up to
heaven in a cloud, while their enemies looked on.

¹³At that very hour there was a severe earthquake and a
tenth of the city collapsed. Seven thousand people were killed
in the earthquake, and the survivors were terrified and gave
glory to the God of heaven.

These verses are the third part of the second woe that
began in chapter 9, verse 13. In the first part the hordes of
hell plagued all people with their temptations and false doctrine. In the second part Jesus commissioned John as a
prophet to take the message of the open scroll to all the
world. In this third and last part of the second woe, we see
what happens to the church and its messengers as it bears
witness to the mystery of God's grace in the New Testament
age. Jesus asked John to measure the temple and observe the
two witnesses at work. In this way John was assured that the
work of sharing the message of the little scroll was not his
alone. Bringing the gospel to the world is the mission of
every believer until the Savior returns.

John was told to measure the temple of God with a measuring reed. The one who gave John this direction was either
the mighty angel, Jesus (10:9), or the voice from heaven,
God (10:8). By measuring the temple, John was to determine
its size and count the worshipers. In very brief summary, this
part of John's vision parallels Ezekiel's lengthy vision of
measuring the temple (Ezekiel 40–48).

This temple is not the one in heaven that John has mentioned twice before (3:12; 7:15). This temple is in the "holy
city" (verse 2) and is thus the temple at Jerusalem, a temple
on earth. In three of his letters, Paul calls the holy Christian
church a temple (2 Corinthians 6:16; Ephesians 2:21; 2 Thessalonians 2:4), and in another letter he says that believers on
earth belong to a spiritual temple, "the Jerusalem that is

above" (Galatians 4:26). The temple of God here also pictures believers on earth.

The temple at Jerusalem had two main sections, the inner sanctuary and the outer court. Jesus uses this as a way to picture the Christian church on earth. There are those who worship in the inner sanctuary, the elect, and those who associate themselves with the temple but never proceed beyond the outer court. Martin Luther taught that the church has both an invisible and a visible aspect. The world looks at the Christian church and sees only one, visible structure. But God looks at the heart (1 Samuel 16:7) and distinguishes between the true believers in the sanctuary and the hypocrites who belong in the outer court.

John is told to "exclude the outer court" from his measurement of the temple (verse 2). Although the outer court is visibly attached to the temple, those with only an external relationship to the church do not share Jesus' commission to witness to the world. The outer court "has been given to the Gentiles" (verse 2). Just as the temple is figurative, so are the Gentiles. This word does not refer to non-Jews, but to non-Christians outwardly attached to the church. These "Gentiles" have no share in the work of the two witnesses (verse 3) and actually harm the church's gospel witness to the world: "They will trample on the holy city for 42 months" (verse 2).

The "42 months" in verse 2 is the same amount of time as the "1,260 days" in verse 3. Both add up to three and a half years. This time period will be mentioned again in the next two chapters. Each time it occurs, the context makes it clear that it refers to God's church in the New Testament era. In this case, three and a half years covers the time from when John was commissioned to prophesy the contents of the open scroll until the church's two witnesses are called to heaven.

110

Perhaps because of the figurative nature of his visions, John never says simply, "three and a half years." Instead, he designates this time in terms of days and months and, in the next chapter, "a time, times and half a time" (12:14). Since the number 3 appears in Revelation as a symbolic number for God and the number 4, as the people on earth, we might understand 7 to signify God's interaction with his people. Seven years might picture the total time that God meets the people on earth with his promise, three and a half years under the Old Testament covenant and three and a half under the New Testament. If we remember that John is recording the words of Jesus, we will be satisfied with what we know for sure. This three-and-a-half-year period, regardless of how it is designated, refers to the whole New Testament age.

Throughout this age God will give his church two faithful witnesses (verse 3). The fact that they are dressed in sackcloth (verse 3) reminds us of the low esteem messengers of the gospel seem to have in the eyes of the world. The presence of two witnesses probably does not in any way signify the number of witnesses the church sends forth through the ages, although they are comparatively few in number.

The NIV translation calls these witnesses "men" in verse 6, but that word does not actually appear in the original language of John's writing. The witnesses are never called men, and John never identifies them as believers. It is more likely that the number 2 indicates the nature of the message rather than the number of messengers. John has twice spoken of the two-edged sword of the Word coming from Jesus' mouth (1:16; 2:12). The sword of the gospel's witness cuts in two directions. "Whoever believes and is baptized will be saved, but whoever does not believe will be condemned" (Mark 16:16). Although the gospel is one message of Christ, it appears in differing ways to those who respond to it. Paul wrote, "For we are to God the aroma of Christ among those who are being saved and to those who are perishing. To the one we are the smell of death; to the other, the fragrance of life" (2 Corinthians 2:15,16).

In verse 4 the two witnesses are called "the two olive trees and the two lampstands." The picture of the two olive trees is taken from Zechariah's vision (Zechariah 4:1-7). In that vision, God made it clear that his will on earth would be done "not by might nor by power, but by [his] Spirit" (Zechariah 4:6). The success of the witness of his church lies in the power of God's message, not in his messengers. Earlier, Jesus explained that the seven lampstands were the seven churches of Asia Minor (1:20). These have passed from history. The two witnesses, however, are the "two lampstands that stand before the Lord of the earth." These two witnesses of God's message will remain until the Lord returns.

When he was speaking of the last days, Jesus promised, "Heaven and earth will pass away, but my words will never pass away" (Matthew 24:35). Jesus repeats this promise in a different way in verses 5 and 6. Terrible things happen to those who think they can stand in the way of the gospel. The fire that comes from the mouths of the witnesses is the message of God's judgment on those who do not believe. The shut-up sky (verse 6) reminds us of the drought Elijah prophesied against the idolatrous Ahab (1 Kings 17:1). The bloody waters and the plagues remind us of the judgments God gave Moses to bring against Pharaoh (Exodus 7–11).

Those who oppose the message of the gospel may personally face destruction or be deterred by general disasters. The natural world that was brought into existence by God's powerful word stands at his command to protect the interests of his worldwide witness until the end of time. Many times infidels and persecutors have declared the gospel dead, only to find themselves removed from the scene of history by the hand of God.

The two witnesses eventually finish their testimony. Through Matthew's pen Jesus has already indicated when this will take place: "This gospel of the kingdom will be preached in the whole world as a testimony to all nations, and then the end will come" (Matthew 24:14). If we keep this time frame in mind, the pictures in the next few verses will be easier to understand.

Note that "the beast that comes up from the Abyss" (verse 7) attacks the two witnesses after they have completed their testimony. The time when the gospel message has completed its course is determined by God, who sends out his Word, and not by its enemies. The beast from the Abyss is the same as "the angel of the Abyss" (9:11). Satan and his influence through his many spirit and human agents overpower and silence the witnesses.

The bodies of the witnesses lie, seemingly dead, in the street of the great city (verse 8). The great city is Jerusalem. The NIV translation says that Jerusalem is "figuratively" called Sodom and Egypt (verse 8). The Greek actually says, "in a spiritual sense." Spiritually speaking, Sodom and Egypt are both known for refusing God's message and suffering God's judgment for it. Together they stand for the resistance of immorality and worldly power to the gospel. John adds a description of Jerusalem as the place "their Lord was crucified" (verse 8). The Lord was crucified in Jerusalem for the spiritual Sodomites and Egyptians who persistently resist his gospel.

The inhabitants of the earth "will gloat over" the two witnesses as they lie lifeless in the street (verse 10). They refuse them the dignity of burial as a sign of spite. They celebrate by sending gifts to one another. They are falsely relieved that they won't have to listen any more to the judgments the two witnesses spoke against their immorality and unbelief.

The voice of God is apparently silenced, but only for a very short time. The "three and a half days" the two witnesses lie silent (verse 11) is very brief compared to the three and a half years of the New Testament age. This, however, does not provide us with an exact time frame for the last days. We cannot say that there will be a time before the end when the Word of God is completely silent. Jesus' promises (Matthew 24:14,35) lead us to believe otherwise. It is better to see the three and half days as the relatively short time the unrepentant have to gloat before the end comes for all of them.

The events in verses 11 to 13 take place "after the three and a half days" (verse 11). Those who thought they had stopped God's witnesses will see them revived. Jesus said, "There is a judge for the one who rejects me and does not accept my words; that very word which I spoke will condemn him at the last day" (John 12:48). Although verses 11 to 13 may appear to describe the last days before the final judgment, they more likely describe the judgment itself.

The unbelievers will stand in terror at the final judgment when they realize the witnesses they thought they had silenced have become their judges. In this vision God has called his gospel back to himself. But it does not return to him empty; it accomplished what he desired and achieved the purpose for which he sent it (Isaiah 55:11). "At that very hour" (verse 13) the destruction of the earth as we know it will take place. The ones who were killed as well as the survivors must face the judgment. The survivors were "terrified and gave glory to the God of heaven" (verse 13). This is not the kind of praise that comes from faith. It is the reluctant praise that the rebellious will be forced to give to God at the

Last Day. "Every eye will see him, even those who pierced him" (1:7) and "every tongue [will] confess that Jesus Christ is Lord, to the glory of God the Father" (Philippians 2:11).

The seventh trumpet: the third woe

¹⁴The second woe has passed; the third woe is coming soon.
¹⁵The seventh angel sounded his trumpet, and there were loud voices in heaven, which said:

"The kingdom of the world has become
    the kingdom of our Lord and of his Christ,
    and he will reign for ever and ever."

¹⁶And the twenty-four elders, who were seated on their thrones before God, fell on their faces and worshiped God, ¹⁷saying:

"We give thanks to you, Lord God Almighty,
    the One who is and who was,
because you have taken your great power
    and have begun to reign.
¹⁸ The nations were angry;
    and your wrath has come.
The time has come for judging the dead,
    and for rewarding your servants the prophets
and your saints and those who reverence your name,
    both small and great—
and for destroying those who destroy the earth."

¹⁹Then God's temple in heaven was opened, and within his temple was seen the ark of his covenant. And there came flashes of lightning, rumblings, peals of thunder, an earthquake and a great hailstorm.

The end of the second woe and the beginning of the third changes the scene from earth to heaven. The events of the third woe, however, take place at the same time as the events at the end of the second. It is the day of judgment.

115

The third woe is a description of the joy in heaven at the prospect of God's final justice and the believer's ultimate victory. Why is such a celebration called a "woe"? The believer finds nothing scary in the last woe. But the three woes, including the believer's joy on the day of judgment, should strike fear in those who remain unrepentant in the last days.

The third woe is the seventh part of the vision of the seven trumpets that began in chapter 8. Each of the seven parts of this vision was introduced by an angel with a trumpet. When the last of the seven trumpets had sounded, John heard loud voices in heaven (verse 15). This seventh angel was already mentioned in the second woe (10:7). His trumpet signals that the mystery of God is accomplished. Now all the wonderful things that God promises his people in the gospel will be fully revealed.

The loud voices in heaven praise God as "our Lord" (verse 15). This means that these unidentified voices belong not to divine beings but to created ones. Because the response to their song of praise is spoken by the elders who represent believers, this word of praise may have been spoken by an angelic choir. Their loud voices reflect their joy.

They sing, "The kingdom of the world has become the kingdom of our Lord and of his Christ" (verse 15). This present world has always been a part of Christ's kingdom. Even now he is reigning over all things. Paul wrote, "He must reign until he has put all his enemies under his feet" (1 Corinthians 15:25). Yet as long as Satan influences the world, Christ's absolute rule is not apparent to all. Judgment day, however, will usher in a new age. On the Last Day, the answer to our daily prayer, "Your kingdom come," will be clearly seen by both friend and foe alike. The influence of Christ and his spiritual reign will be unopposed. The never-ending freedom from sorrow believers will enjoy (21:4) stems from the fact that Jesus "will reign for ever and ever" (verse 15).

The elders who sit on their thrones (verse 16) represent all believers who have received the crown of life (see 4:4). Judgment day is God's answer to their plea "How long?" (6:10). They worshiped God by lying flat on the ground with their faces down. By this they show they are undeserving of this victory and completely dependent on God's power. Then they put their humble actions into words of thanks (verse 17). They thank God because he has "begun to reign" (verse 17). This does not mean he did not reign before judgment day, but it means even the devils and the unrepentant will have to acknowledge God's rule.

The same double-edged sword of God's two gospel witnesses (see 11:3) that finished its testimony on earth (11:7) has returned to heaven and becomes the standard God uses in the final judgment (see 11:12). God's time has come for "rewarding" and "destroying" (verse 18). The prophets of the Old and New Testaments will be rewarded for their faithful witness in the face of unbelief and persecution. Beside them at God's right hand will be the saints who continued to honor God's name amid the world's blasphemy. The "saints" and "those who reverence" God's name (verse 18) are both descriptions of believers.

"The nations" (verse 18) are the unbelieving majority in the world. They were angry because the two witnessing prophets tormented them with their warnings of impending judgment (11:10). But their anger was only "storing up wrath" against themselves (Romans 2:5). God's righteous anger will destroy them because they destroyed the earth. The first six trumpets of this vision (8:6–11:13) have demonstrated that the sin and false teaching spawned by the devil

117

wreaks havoc on the natural world as well as the spiritual world. For this there will be a final accounting.

The third and last woe ends with a dramatic picture of the beginning of judgment day. The events of verse 19 correspond to chapter 11, verses 11 to 13. "God's temple in heaven was opened" (verse 19) means that God opened it for all the people on earth to see. This is not the temple in Jerusalem in chapter 11 that symbolized believers on earth. Heaven has no temple, as John will explain later (21:22). This temple is a symbol of God's presence among his people. The judgment is about to begin, and God is opening the doors of the courtroom. The "judging the dead" (verse 18) will take place in a venue where God favors his people.

The two witnesses called back to heaven (11:12) and the visible ark of the covenant in heaven (verse 19) symbolize the same thing: the gospel promise that God proclaimed on earth until the end. The ark of the covenant in the Old Testament temple was the assurance of the promises God made to his people and of his presence among them. Although that ark was lost, the promise of God that stood behind it endures and will be uncovered again at the Last Day.

On the Last Day, the promises of God simultaneously bring joy to the faithful and fear to the unrepentant. The foreboding storm and the hail (verse 19) are pictures of God's wrath against the unbelieving. The lightning and thunder remind us of the presence of God on Mount Sinai (Exodus 19). The hail recalls God's plague against the Egyptians (Exodus 9:22; see 11:8). The earthquake parallels Jesus' warnings about the natural disasters preceding the judgment (Matthew 24:7; see 11:13).

This is the end of the third woe and the end of the vision of the seven trumpets. The terrible warnings about punishment for stubborn sinners are for the unrepentant. To the extent that the believer's faith is not perfected, these warnings are for him too. Our lazy sinful nature must be crucified anew each day with the warnings of the law. As we prepare for the last days, we come before God, falling on our faces, and seek refuge alone in Jesus Christ.

VISION OF THE SEVEN VISIONS
(12:1–15:8)

The first vision: the dragon and the Child

12 A great and wondrous sign appeared in heaven: a woman clothed with the sun, with the moon under her feet and a crown of twelve stars on her head. ²She was pregnant and cried out in pain as she was about to give birth. ³Then another sign appeared in heaven: an enormous red dragon with seven heads and ten horns and seven crowns on his heads. ⁴His tail swept a third of the stars out of the sky and flung them to the earth. The dragon stood in front of the woman who was about to give birth, so that he might devour her child the moment it was born. ⁵She gave birth to a son, a male child, who will rule all the nations with an iron scepter. And her child was snatched up to God and to his throne. ⁶The woman fled into the desert to a place prepared for her by God, where she might be taken care of for 1,260 days.

⁷And there was war in heaven. Michael and his angels fought against the dragon, and the dragon and his angels fought back. ⁸But he was not strong enough, and they lost their place in heaven. ⁹The great dragon was hurled down— that ancient serpent called the devil, or Satan, who leads the whole world astray. He was hurled to the earth, and his angels with him.

¹⁰Then I heard a loud voice in heaven say:

"Now have come the salvation and the power and the
 kingdom of our God,
 and the authority of his Christ.
For the accuser of our brothers,
 who accuses them before our God day and night,
 has been hurled down.

"That ancient serpent called the devil" (12:9)

¹¹ They overcame him
  by the blood of the Lamb
  and by the word of their testimony;
  they did not love their lives so much
   as to shrink from death.
¹² Therefore rejoice, you heavens
  and you who dwell in them!
But woe to the earth and the sea,
  because the devil has gone down to you!
He is filled with fury,
  because he knows that his time is short."

¹³When the dragon saw that he had been hurled to the earth, he pursued the woman who had given birth to the male child. ¹⁴The woman was given the two wings of a great eagle, so that she might fly to the place prepared for her in the desert, where she would be taken care of for a time, times and half a time, out of the serpent's reach. ¹⁵Then from his mouth the serpent spewed water like a river, to overtake the woman and sweep her away with the torrent. ¹⁶But the earth helped the woman by opening its mouth and swallowing the river that the dragon had spewed out of his mouth. ¹⁷Then the dragon was enraged at the woman and went off to make war against the rest of her offspring—those who obey God's commandments and hold to the testimony of Jesus.

13 And the dragon stood on the shore of the sea.

Chapter 12 marks the beginning of John's fourth vision, the vision of the seven visions. There is no formal introduction to this vision as there was at the beginning of the last two. Still, the subject matter makes it clear that a transition from the events at the close of the last chapter has occurred. It is important to note this transition so that we understand the time frame in which the visions take place. This fourth vision covers the same time that the second and third visions did. The vision of the seven visions depicts events from the beginning of the New Testament age until the last days and the final judgment.

The first of the seven visions is announced by "a great and wondrous sign" in heaven (verse 1). John saw a woman who "was about to give birth" (verse 2). When we read later that she gave birth to a male child that the devil sought to destroy (verses 4,5), we might be tempted to identify this woman with Mary, the mother of Jesus. The description of this woman, however, rules out that interpretation.

We note in verse 6 that God will take care of this woman for 1,260 days. This is the three and a half years we identified earlier as a symbol of the New Testament age (see 11:3). In verse 12 this woman's offspring are identified as "those who obey God's commandments and hold to the testimony of Jesus." From this it is clear that the woman represents the church, God's people on earth.

Identifying the woman as the church fits with the description of her in verse 1. She is "clothed with the sun." Through faith she shares the perfection of the Savior, whose face shone like the sun at his transfiguration. The moon under her feet reminds us that believers share in Christ's reign, including his rule of the universe. "You have been given fullness in Christ, who is the head over every power and authority" (Colossians 2:10; see 2 Timothy 2:12). The crown of 12 stars on her head convincingly marks this woman as the church. In Revelation the number 12 and its multiples represent the church (see 4:4; 7:4-8). Her crown is the crown of victory that all the faithful receive (see 2:10; 3:11). The stars also may signify the spiritual leaders of the church (see 1:20).

Then John saw "an enormous red dragon" (verse 3). Red is the color of bloodshed and death (see 6:4). The huge size of the dragon shows its great potential for inflicting harm. In verse 9 this dragon is identified as Satan. Satan's seven heads indicate the deceitful way he influences people. The number 7 usually indicates God's activity on behalf of his people. Yet Paul writes, "Satan himself masquerades as an angel of light" (2 Corinthians 11:14). The deceitful nature of his seven heads is exaggerated by his seven "crowns." For Satan's "crowns" John used a Greek word entirely different from the one he used for the woman's "crown," the crown of victory, in verse 1. The dragon's "crown" is a diadem, a presumptuous headpiece once worn by ancient rulers who wanted to be revered as gods.

Horns symbolize power (see 5:6). The number 10 is the number for something that God limits (see 2:10). The horns here, as in chapter 17, verses 7 and 12, may indicate the earthly rulers through whom Satan exercises his influence. Satan's power is also illustrated by the sweep of the dragon's tail through the sky. Stars signify leaders. The stars that fell under Satan's influence remind us of the angels he drew with him when he was cast out of heaven, "the angels who did not keep their positions of authority but abandoned their own home" (Jude 6).

The woman gave birth to "a male child, who will rule all the nations with an iron scepter" (verse 5). David prophesied that the coming Savior would rule his enemies with an "iron scepter" (Psalm 2:9). This male child is Jesus. The fact that in this vision Jesus is the woman's child by no means forces us to identify the woman with the virgin Mary. The Bible says Jesus is Eve's offspring (Genesis 3:15), and the genealogical charts in Matthew 1 and Luke 3 prove that Jesus was physically descended from the people he came to save. The mother of this child signifies not a particular human progenitor, but the human nature of all the people who receive him as their Savior.

124

The dragon knew why the child had come, and Satan stood ready to destroy Jesus. "The dragon stood in front of the woman who was about to give birth, so that he might devour her child the moment it was born" (verse 4). The wording here might suggest the attempt of one of Satan's "horns," King Herod, to kill the Christ Child. The very next event in this vision, however, is God snatching the child up to heaven. So, although Satan's attempts to destroy Jesus began at his birth, all the devil's efforts to stop Jesus throughout his time on earth are symbolized here. The temptation in the wilderness, the many demon possessions, the early attempts of the Jews to stone him, and the crucifixion are all pictured in the dragon's attempt to devour the child.

John relates Jesus' ascension to God's right hand with little symbolism. He writes that the woman's child "was snatched up to God and to his throne" (verse 5). Except for the fact that John calls Jesus a "child" at the time of his ascension (verse 5), his description of Christ's exaltation is literally true. Twice before, John pictured Jesus at the center of the throne of God (5:6; 7:17). Mark records that Jesus "was taken up into heaven and he sat at the right hand of God" (Mark 16:19). Both the throne and the right hand are symbols of regal authority.

John calls Jesus a child three times. The number 3 hints at his divinity, and the word "child" emphasizes his humanity. Jesus was true God from all eternity and, as God, possessed all divine power and authority. That Jesus is called a child, even at the time of his ascension, reminds us that his ascent to the throne was the exaltation of his human nature.

Verse 6 eliminates any thought that the woman in this vision is the virgin Mary: "The woman fled into the desert to a place prepared for her by God, where she might be taken care of for 1,260 days." The three and a half years symbolize the entire New Testament age. The woman in this vision is the church. Believers live out their existence in the wilderness of this world under the protecting hand of God.

Three scenes are in this first vision of seven visions. Scene 2, which begins at verse 6, takes us from earth to the spiritual realm. In Greek the word for heaven can also mean "sky," similar to the English *heaven* and *the heavens*. The "war in heaven" (verse 7), then, should not be identified with God's expulsion of Satan from heaven shortly after creation. Although many understand these verses to picture that event, two things lead us away from that interpretation.

First, the battle here is between Michael and his angels and the dragon and his angels. At the beginning of creation, however, Satan's rebellion was against God, and God expelled him from heaven. Saints Peter and Jude both say that God cast the evil angels "into gloomy dungeons" (2 Peter 2:4) and has kept them "in darkness, bound with everlasting chains" (Jude 6). Second, the time frame for all three scenes of this vision is the New Testament age. Satan's original rebellion happened at the beginning of the Old Testament.

Where and when did this battle occur? The place was what John calls the "sky." Paul called Satan "the ruler of the kingdom of the air" (Ephesians 2:2). John writes later that the angel with the everlasting gospel was in "midair" (14:6). Paul told the Ephesians that their real battle was not against flesh and blood, but "against the powers of this dark world and against the spiritual forces of evil in the heavenly realms" (Ephesians 6:12). We might call this battlefield the spiritual realm, the place where the battle for men's souls takes place.

The time of this battle cannot be pinpointed. We can be sure, however, that the power for every victory over the dragon was ensured by Jesus' death and resurrection. As

126

Jesus set his eyes toward the cross, he said, "Now the prince of this world will be driven out" (John 12:31). When he rose from the dead, he announced his victory over the spirits in hell (1 Peter 3:19). "Having disarmed the powers and authorities, he made a public spectacle of them, triumphing over them by the cross" (Colossians 2:15).

The dragon "was not strong enough, and they lost their place in heaven" (verse 8). This does not mean that the devil ever had a place in heaven since he was cast out by God. "Heaven" again refers to the spiritual realm. The devil once had "a place," that is, some significant sway in the spiritual realm. Jesus' death and resurrection, however, hurled Satan to the earth (verse 9). He is no longer a dominating power in the spiritual realm, and his work is restricted to tempting people on earth. This may explain the abatement of physical demon possession after Christ's ascension.

In one sense the battle between Michael and the dragon is waged to a lesser degree every time a soul is reclaimed from Satan's grasp. Jesus said, "There is rejoicing in the presence of the angels of God over one sinner who repents" (Luke 15:10). Angels are involved in the battle for souls throughout the New Testament age. When the 72 returned with joy over the success of the gospel, Jesus told them, "I saw Satan fall like lightning from heaven" (Luke 10:18).

There was joy in heaven when the devil and his angels were hurled to the earth. John heard a loud voice in heaven praising God (verse 10). The voice is not identified, but it speaks for all believers and the holy angels. Its loud volume indicates the importance of its message. This stanza of praise supports the thought that the war between Michael and the dragon took place in connection with Jesus' death. The content of the three verses of this praise (verses 10-12) corresponds in time with Christ's crucifixion and ascension.

"Now have come the salvation and the power and the kingdom of our God" (verse 10). Now that Jesus has won his victory, three of God's saving influences come on the scene in a more dramatic way than they did in the Old Testament. God's salvation for his people is no longer a promise but a proclamation of an accomplished blessing. God publicly displayed his power over Satan by the resurrection. God's kingdom is his ruling influence on behalf of his people, especially as he reigns in our hearts with the gospel. The beginning of the New Testament marks the time when this kingdom will be extended to all the world as never before.

The "authority of his Christ" (verse 10) is the authority by which he commissioned us to carry God's salvation, power and kingdom to the whole world. Jesus said, "All authority in heaven and on earth has been given to me. Therefore go and make disciples of all nations" (Matthew 28:18,19). Jesus told the 72 when they returned, "I have given you authority to trample on snakes and scorpions and to overcome all the power of the enemy" (Luke 10:19). Jesus was able to convey that authority to us because, at the time of his ascension, the great battle against Satan was over. "The accuser of our brothers, who accuses them before our God day and night, has been hurled down" (verse 10).

The loud voice in heaven thanked God because his people overcame Satan "by the blood of the Lamb and by the word of their testimony" (verse 11). Satan's influence is curbed when we receive the power of Jesus through faith and share his victory with others. The early Christian martyrs demonstrated that they understood God's twofold purpose for their lives. In pursuit of these two purposes for Christian life, "they did not love their lives so much as to shrink from death" (verse 11). Our lifetimes also are a time of grace to come to faith in Jesus and to give testimony to his Word.

The last verse of praise (verse 12) also points to the crucifixion as the time when the great battle between Michael and
the dragon was fought. This transitional verse reflects joy
over Jesus' victory but ends with the warning that, although
the war has been won, the battles will continue. The devil is
limited, but he is not powerless. God has confined his area of
influence to the earth and the sea. God has limited the time
Satan has left to dispense his evil. The believer's joy over
Christ's victory is coupled with constant vigilance. The devil
is like a roaring lion. "He is filled with fury" (verse 12).
Those who rejoice in the "heavens" are those who are safe in
the spiritual realm. Those who hold by faith to Christ's crucifixion remain in that sphere of influence from which Satan
has lost his place.

Verse 13 begins the third and last scene of the first of the
seven visions. The sequence of these three scenes strengthens
our faith. In the first scene the great dragon attacks the child,
Jesus, but is frustrated by Christ's ascension to the throne of
God. In the second scene the great dragon is defeated in the
spiritual realm by the power of Christ's crucifixion and resurrection. Now this furious dragon, a two-time loser, turns his
wrath on Christ's church.

When the dragon saw that he was no match for Jesus and
his holy angels, "he pursued the woman who had given birth
to the male child" (verse 13). We have already identified this
woman as the church, God's people in the New Testament age
(see 12:1). "The two wings of a great eagle" (verse 14) represent the power of the double victory of Christ and his angels,
won in the first two scenes of this vision. Jesus keeps his
church in the spiritual realm, the "place" from which Satan
has been deposed. God prepared this area of safety where his
people will be "out of the serpent's reach." There God will
take care of his church for "a time, times and half a time."

This is the three and a half years that John has used (11:2,3; 12:6) to signify the duration of the New Testament age.

The safety God gives his church of the New Testament does not deter Satan's attempts to hurt her. The devil will try to "overtake the woman and sweep her away with the torrent" (verse 15). This torrent is the flood of temptation, false teaching, and persecution the devil unleashes against the church. "But the earth helped the woman" (verse 16). At his ascension Jesus was given authority on earth. Though the devil's activity is confined to the earth, Jesus is still in control. "The gates of Hades [hell] will not overcome" his church (Matthew 16:18). The image of the earth "swallowing" the devil's torrent (verse 16) envisions all the ways Jesus may blunt the attacks of Satan on behalf of his people.

Frustrated in his attempt to kill the child, then stripped of his authority in the spiritual realm, the dragon was "enraged" (verse 17) at the woman. He saw that he would never be able to destroy the "woman," that is, the whole church. So the dragon turned his attack to individual believers. He "went off to make war against the rest of her offspring—those who obey God's commandments and hold to the testimony of Jesus." The way he wages this attack on the members of the church is the subject of the next two visions (13:2-18). As the dragon contemplated what forces to deploy against believers, he "stood on the shore of the sea" (13:1).

The second vision: the beast from the sea

And I saw a beast coming out of the sea. He had ten horns and seven heads, with ten crowns on his horns, and on each head a blasphemous name. [2]The beast I saw resembled a leopard, but had feet like those of a bear and a mouth like that of a lion. The dragon gave the beast his power and his throne and great authority. [3]One of the heads of the beast seemed to have

had a fatal wound, but the fatal wound had been healed. The whole world was astonished and followed the beast. ⁴Men worshiped the dragon because he had given authority to the beast, and they also worshiped the beast and asked, "Who is like the beast? Who can make war against him?"

⁵The beast was given a mouth to utter proud words and blasphemies and to exercise his authority for forty-two months. ⁶He opened his mouth to blaspheme God, and to slander his name and his dwelling place and those who live in heaven. ⁷He was given power to make war against the saints and to conquer them. And he was given authority over every tribe, people, language and nation. ⁸All inhabitants of the earth will worship the beast—all whose names have not been written in the book of life belonging to the Lamb that was slain from the creation of the world.

⁹He who has an ear, let him hear.

¹⁰ If anyone is to go into captivity,
    into captivity he will go.
If anyone is to be killed with the sword,
    with the sword he will be killed.

This calls for patient endurance and faithfulness on the part of the saints.

The second of the seven visions shows us the first of two agents Satan summons to help him attack God's people, the "beast coming out of the sea" (verse 1). Just like the red dragon (12:3), this beast has seven heads and ten horns. But the beast wears its "crowns" on its horns, not on its heads. The ten horns represent the limited power of the devil (see 12:3). The crowns are not the believers' crowns of victory but pretentious diadems worn by those who seek to be revered as gods. The blasphemous names on each of the beast's heads mimic and mock the true God. Although 7 usually represents God's work among his people, the seven heads of the beast deceitfully picture him as a friend of believers.

This beast from the sea is much like the four beasts in Daniel's vision (Daniel 7). Daniel's beasts resembled various ferocious animals, and John's beast from the sea has many of the features of beasts of prey (verse 2). John does not tell us what his beast from the sea represents, but Daniel's interpretation of his four beasts helps us identify it.

The beast from the sea is an agent and ally of Satan: "The dragon gave the beast his power and his throne and great authority" (verse 2). Since Satan's sphere of influence was confined to earth (see 12:9), the authority he conveys to the beast is an earthly power. The beast's ten crowns are another hint to his identity. The number 10 signifies a limit that God imposes, and the diadems he wears indicate the claim worldly rulers make to deity. The beast from the sea, then, symbolizes the governmental powers established by God but used by Satan against the church in the New Testament age.

Daniel's interpretation of his four beasts reinforces our identification of John's beast from the sea. Daniel wrote, "The four great beasts are four kingdoms that will rise from the earth. But the saints of the Most High will receive the kingdom and will possess it forever—yes, for ever and ever" (Daniel 7:17,18). Daniel's four beasts prophesied four specific government powers. John speaks of only one beast and does not identify a specific world ruler because his beast stands for all the world governments Satan uses against the church in the New Testament age. Yet like Daniel's interpretation, John's prevailing message is that God's saints will inherit his kingdom in spite of all the earthly powers Satan uses against them.

Satan did not create world government. "The authorities that exist have been established by God" (Romans 13:1). Yet

Satan often uses God's creation for his evil purposes. The dragon in John's vision did not create the sea, but he evokes the beast from the sea to do his destructive work on the church. Christians must live in two kingdoms, Luther said, under spiritual and civil authority. Believers live in the world and recognize the legitimate right of earthly powers to require our obedience. "Everyone must submit himself to the governing authorities" (Romans 13:1). At the same time, we understand that secular power can be corrupted by Satan. When the devil forces his will on us through government, we remember that we are members of God's kingdom first. Then we say with the apostles, "We must obey God rather than men!" (Acts 5:29).

"One of the heads of the beast seemed to have had a fatal wound, but the fatal wound had been healed" (verse 3). The beast's fatal head wound might lead us to think of when God told the serpent in the Garden of Eden that Eve's seed, the coming Savior, would crush his head (Genesis 3:15). In John's vision, however, the fatal wound is to the beast's head, not to Satan's. It is better, then, to understood the fatal head wound to the beast as a general sign. New Testament history has demonstrated that sometimes civil government, even under Satan's influence, injures the devil more than it helps him.

Satan influences secular authority to make it something God did not create it to be. Down through the ages, more people have looked to their government than to Jesus as savior. Most of the world depends solely on government to provide economic welfare, physical protection, education, and acts of charity. Revolutionaries rely on a change in human authority to give them what only divine authority can guarantee. Unbelievers seek the physical benefits of government to the neglect of their spiritual needs. The vision of the whole world following the beast and worshiping the dragon pictures this idolatry (verses 3,4). Many patriots, not realizing that the beast is an agent of the dragon, have sought God's favor through civic duty instead of through faith in Christ. When that happens, the devil wins. His agent, the beast, has accomplished its destructive mission.

Satan will abuse the pervasive power of secular government "for forty-two months" (verse 5), that is, throughout the New Testament age (see 11:2). At times, atheistic regimes will claim divine power. Some will officially establish pagan religions and forbid true worship. Others will physically persecute Christians. This is what John means by "proud words and blasphemies . . . slander . . . war against the saints" (verses 5-7). "All the inhabitants of the earth will worship the beast" (verse 8). Satan's sway over secular power extends throughout time among "every tribe, people, language and nation" (verse 7). Christians can expect that when their government abuses its power to hurt them, the general populace will join in that abuse.

The elect, however, will not join the mad rush to deify secular authority. Their names are "written in the book of life" (verse 8; see 3:5). By faith they trust that their future with God is secure, no matter what men may do to them. They belong "to the Lamb that was slain from the creation of the world." Forgiveness was a reality before Jesus died on the cross. Thousands of years before Jesus was born, when God promised Eve that her seed would defeat Satan, faith trusted that the Lamb was already slain. Every believer has such confidence that God keeps his word. Through John's pen Jesus invites us to hold on to his promises during the last days: "He who has an ear, let him hear" (verse 9).

Believers who live simultaneously under God's authority and man's government must understand this vision of the beast from the sea. The beast is not civil government, but the abuse of political power by Satan and his allies. This distinction helps us walk the fine line between giving to Caesar the things that are Caesar's and to God what belongs to him (Mark 12:17). This vision, then, is not a call to civil disobedience. When government shows itself to be the beast from the sea, we will obey God without disobeying earthly authorities. That means holding to the truth and humbly accepting the consequences. John explains, "If anyone is to go into captivity, into captivity he will go. If anyone is to be killed with the sword, with the sword he will be killed" (verse 10).

The vision of the beast from the sea invites our long-term trust in the face of short-term loss. The devil wins battles, but Jesus won the war. We are confident that no matter what we suffer under earthly rule, "the saints of the Most High will receive the kingdom and will possess it forever—yes, for ever and ever" (Daniel 7:18). "This calls for patient endurance and faithfulness on the part of the saints" (verse 10).

The third vision: the beast from the earth

¹¹**Then I saw another beast, coming out of the earth. He had two horns like a lamb, but he spoke like a dragon. ¹²He exercised all the authority of the first beast on his behalf, and made the earth and its inhabitants worship the first beast, whose fatal wound had been healed. ¹³And he performed great and miraculous signs, even causing fire to come down from heaven to earth in full view of men. ¹⁴Because of the signs he was given power to do on behalf of the first beast, he deceived the inhabitants of the earth. He ordered them to set up an image in honor of the beast who was wounded by the sword and yet lived. ¹⁵He was given power to give breath to the image of the first beast, so that it could speak and cause all who refused to worship the image to be killed. ¹⁶He also forced everyone, small and great, rich and poor, free and slave, to receive a mark on his right hand or on his forehead, ¹⁷so that no one could buy or**

sell unless he had the mark, which is the name of the beast or the number of his name.

[18]This calls for wisdom. If anyone has insight, let him calculate the number of the beast, for it is man's number. His number is 666.

The third of the seven visions pictures another agent of Satan, the beast coming out of the earth (verse 11). This beast had two horns like a lamb. This threat to the church poses as Jesus, the Lamb of God. We see through his deceit, however, because John has pictured the real Lamb with seven horns (5:6). This beast's treachery is not well masked because when he speaks "like a dragon" (verse 11), he reveals himself as an ally of Satan.

The identity of this beast becomes clearer when we watch what he does. Jesus said, "Watch out for false prophets. They come to you in sheep's clothing, but inwardly they are ferocious wolves. By their fruit you will recognize them" (Matthew 7:15,16). The fruit of a false prophet is his message and its effect on his hearers. The beast from the earth demonstrates by his actions that he is in league with the beast from the sea. He "made the earth and its inhabitants worship the first beast, whose fatal wound had been healed" (verse 12; see 13:3).

Other clues to his identity follow. He "performed great and miraculous signs" (verse 13) and led people into idolatry (verse 14). These activities of the beast correspond to Paul's description of the "man of lawlessness" (2 Thessalonians 2:3). "The coming of the lawless one will be in accordance with the work of Satan displayed in all kinds of counterfeit miracles. . . . He will oppose and will exalt himself over everything that is called God or is worshiped, so that he sets himself up in God's temple, proclaiming himself to be God" (2 Thessalonians 2:9,4).

136

The second beast "was given power to give breath to the image of the first beast" (verse 15). The first beast, the beast from the sea, represented the evil Satan exerts through human government. In partnership with this beast, the beast from the earth provokes world governments to speak against Christians and persecute them.

The mark that this unholy beast forces his followers to wear (verse 16) is a cheap imitation of the seal God puts on his people (see 7:2,3). This mark on the right hand or forehead of the beast's followers indicates that their work and thinking belong to the beast. With this identifying mark and through his unholy alliance with the beast of the sea, the second beast influenced the government to practice economic discrimination against believers.

Taken together, these pictures of the beast provide us with his identity. With his lamb's horns he poses as a representative of the Lamb, but his message sounds like Satan's. He collaborates with worldly authorities in order to harm the real followers of the Lamb. He performs miraculous signs that deceive people into the idolatry of earthly power. He cooperates with human authorities to persecute Christians and cause hardship to those who do not accept his message.

John identifies this beast at the end of the vision (verses 17,18), but with symbolic language. He says the mark of the beast is the name of the beast. In the Bible "name" often means reputation or what is known about a person. This beast, then, may be known from what he teaches. What message in this world masquerades as religion, is preached by false Christs and government powers alike, impresses the majority, destroys the gospel, and leads to the persecution of Christians?

To help us answer this question, John offers one more piece of identification, the beast's number. He says that the beast's mark, his name, and his number are all the same. The number of the beast is 666, "man's number" (verse 18). As 7 stands for God's gospel efforts in the world, 666 signifies a message that comes close to sounding like the gospel but always falls short of it. Man's number is man's religion, the man-made notion that we can save ourselves, the devil's lie that we can earn our own salvation. Work-righteousness is the one religious notion shared among all pagan religions, all false doctrines, and all political systems. It is the self-deceit that if we do our best, God will have to accept us.

The evidence of this beast at work in the New Testament can be seen in various places, but some stand out more than others. The Roman papacy must be included. Our Lutheran Confessions identify that office as the antichrist because it teaches salvation by works, claims to be the vicar of Christ, and has operated in partnership with civil government for most of history. Modern Protestantism's social gospel is also evidence of the beast at work. The New Age Movement and the resurgence of Islamic and oriental philosophies bear the mark of the beast too.

Identifying this beast "calls for wisdom," John writes (verse 18). Spiritual wisdom, the insight gained from Bible-based faith in Christ, is needed to identify the beast outside and inside. We must identify the beast in the world but not stop with that. The beast is the religion of man. He represents the religion of work-righteousness, which lurks within our own souls too—that insidious error that we can earn or contribute to our status with God. Daily sorrow over our sins and our sinful nature—always linked with renewed trust in the blood of the Lamb—will give us wisdom.

The fourth vision: the 144,000 with the Lamb

14 Then I looked, and there before me was the Lamb, standing on Mount Zion, and with him 144,000 who

had his name and his Father's name written on their foreheads. ²And I heard a sound from heaven like the roar of
rushing waters and like a loud peal of thunder. The sound I
heard was like that of harpists playing their harps. ³And they
sang a new song before the throne and before the four living
creatures and the elders. No one could learn the song except
the 144,000 who had been redeemed from the earth. ⁴These
are those who did not defile themselves with women, for they
kept themselves pure. They follow the Lamb wherever he
goes. They were purchased from among men and offered as
firstfruits to God and the Lamb. ⁵No lie was found in their
mouths; they are blameless.

The fourth of the seven visions swept John up to heaven,
away from a world plagued by threatening beasts. As the
scene changes, the time changes too. The third vision viewed
the suffering church before the judgment. This fourth vision
sees the victorious church after the judgment. You can sense
that John's mood changes abruptly as he leaves the vision of
the impostor lamb (13:11) and sees Jesus, the real Lamb, in
front of him (verse 1). John first saw the Lamb when his second vision drew him before the throne of God in heaven (5:6).
John mentions the Lamb a total of 30 times in Revelation.

The Lamb was standing on Mount Zion. Zion was the hill
in the city of Jerusalem on which Solomon's temple was
built. Both Old and New Testament writers use Mount Zion
as a symbol for the church. With Jesus are the "144,000 who
had his name and his Father's name written on their foreheads" (verse 1). John earlier described the 144,000 as the
elect, those who were sealed by God on earth to protect them
from the calamities of the last days (7:4-8).

Those who wore God's seal on their foreheads on earth
wear the name of the Lamb and the Father in heaven. John
recorded Jesus' words "I and the Father are one" in his

Gospel (10:30). Now he sees no inconsistency in reporting that the elect have the name of the Lamb and the Father on their foreheads. God's "name" is his reputation, what he reveals about himself in his Word. Although the Father and the Son are distinct persons of the Trinity and their personal names are different, they are one in essence and what they reveal about themselves to believers is the same.

John heard the sound of a majestic chorus in heaven. The "rushing waters" and the "loud peal of thunder" (verse 2) signify the exuberant joy of the singers. The sound like "harpists playing their harps" (verse 2) reflects the beauty and spiritual harmony of their song. The heavenly chorus "sang a new song" (verse 3). The books of Psalms and Isaiah encourage believers to sing a new song. Both on earth and in heaven this new song thanks God for his salvation (see 5:9). Only the redeemed can learn this song because only they understand the joy of salvation.

The choir of the elect directs its praise to the throne in the company of the four living creatures and the elders. The four living creatures represent the created world, and the 24 elders represent the church (see 4:4). Here, amid the 144,000, the elders may stand for the leaders of the Old and New Testament church.

John describes the 144,000 in heaven for the sake of the elect who are still on this earth. The NIV translation says, "They kept themselves pure" (verse 4). John literally wrote, "They are virgins." Old Testament prophets often spoke of God's church as his bride. Hosea, in particular, pictured the unfaithfulness of God's people as adultery and threatened that God would divorce them. So when John speaks of the elect "who did not defile themselves with women," he is saying that God's people will not lose their faith to idolatry and false teachings. In a spiritual sense, they go to meet their bridegroom in heaven as virgins (see 21:2).

In heaven the bride, the church, follows Jesus wherever he goes. Heaven is the consummation of the bridegroom's promise to his church. When John writes that the church was "purchased from among men," Paul's words come to mind: "Christ loved the church and gave himself up for her . . . by the washing with water through the word, and to present her to himself as a radiant church, without stain or wrinkle or any other blemish, but holy and blameless" (Ephesians 5:25-27).

The Father purchased the church with the blood of the Lamb. Now he presents the elect to himself as "firstfruits" (verse 4). God himself will harvest all the earth at the last judgment (14:16), but he will gather only the firstfruits to himself. John also says of the elect, "No lie was found in their mouths; they are blameless" (verse 5). This refers not to their personal conduct, but to their faith. They did not believe the deceit by which Satan tried to wean them from the truth of the Lamb.

The fifth vision: the three angels

6Then I saw another angel flying in midair, and he had the eternal gospel to proclaim to those who live on the earth—to every nation, tribe, language and people. 7He said in a loud voice, "Fear God and give him glory, because the hour of his judgment has come. Worship him who made the heavens, the earth, the sea and the springs of water."

8A second angel followed and said, "Fallen! Fallen is Babylon the Great, which made all the nations drink the maddening wine of her adulteries."

9A third angel followed them and said in a loud voice: "If anyone worships the beast and his image and receives his mark on the forehead or on the hand, 10he, too, will drink of the wine

of God's fury, which has been poured full strength into the cup of his wrath. He will be tormented with burning sulfur in the presence of the holy angels and of the Lamb. [11]And the smoke of their torment rises for ever and ever. There is no rest day or night for those who worship the beast and his image, or for anyone who receives the mark of his name." [12]This calls for patient endurance on the part of the saints who obey God's commandments and remain faithful to Jesus.

[13]Then I heard a voice from heaven say, "Write: Blessed are the dead who die in the Lord from now on."

"Yes," says the Spirit, "they will rest from their labor, for their deeds will follow them."

John's visions do not always follow in order of time. This vision is another indication of that. In the last vision John was with the elect in heaven following the judgment. This vision takes him back in time to the New Testament age prior to the final judgment.

This is the fifth of the seven visions. In this vision John sees three angels. Many Lutheran writers identify the first angel as Martin Luther. John saw this angel "flying in midair, and he had the eternal gospel to proclaim to those who live on earth" (verse 6). Certainly Dr. Luther, with his clear preaching of the gospel, must be included among those who fulfill this prophetic vision. The church has well chosen verses 6 and 7 as a Scripture reading for the festival of Reformation. Yet it is clear that the setting for this vision is the entire New Testament age. Thus this angel symbolizes every faithful gospel witness from John's writing until the end of the world. He flies "in midair" (verse 6) so that this message will be heard by "every nation, tribe, language and people" (verse 6). His gospel is "eternal" (verse 6) because, even though the time for its proclamation will end, the fulfillment of its promises stretches into eternity.

The angel's message is direct: "Fear God and give him glory, because the hour of his judgment has come" (verse 7). The fear the angel calls for is the fear of faith. It is not fright, but deep respect for God in response to his gospel promises. The psalmist knew this fear of God: "With you there is forgiveness; therefore you are feared" (Psalm 130:4). Giving glory to God is the way believers demonstrate their faith with their lips and in their lives. This call to faith in the eternal gospel is urgent "because the hour of his judgment has come" (verse 7). This does not mean that judgment day is here. Rather, it means the time is short until God judges every sinner. Repentance and faith must not be delayed.

To those who may not respond to his clear gospel call, the angel makes a more general appeal: "Worship him who made the heavens, the earth, the sea and the springs of water." Those who do not feel a need for a Savior from sin should at least begin thinking about the origin of their existence. They will soon face their Creator. If they "seek him and perhaps reach out for him" (Acts 17:27), they may learn, before it is too late, that the Creator sent his Son, the Lamb, for them.

The second angel announced the fall of Babylon. Isaiah uttered a similar prophecy of doom against the ancient city of Babylon: "Babylon has fallen, has fallen! All the images of its gods lie shattered on the ground!" (Isaiah 21:9). Babylon, a marvelous city in the ancient world, oppressed God's people, Israel. But within two hundred years of Isaiah's prophecy, proud Babylon lay in total ruin. It no longer exists.

"Babylon the Great" (verse 8) is a symbol for every proud oppressor of the church. The angel said that Babylon "made all the nations drink the maddening wine of her adulteries" (verse 8). Intoxicated with pride and power, many are led to spiritual adultery by impressive human institutions. The elect do not "defile themselves with women" (verse 4), but con-

143

stant pressure from the church's enemies embitters their stay on earth. The impending destruction of the church's enemies, which strikes fear in the heart of the unrepentant, brings comfort to the faithful.

The first angel proclaimed the gospel in the New Testament age (verse 6). The second angel announced the coming judgment (verse 8). Now a third angel announces the outcome of the judgment. There will be eternal punishment for those who worshiped the beast (verse 9). Two beasts were mentioned in chapter 13, the beast from the sea and the beast from the earth. The reference here is to the beast from the earth (see 13:16). The beast from the earth represents the destructive heresy that we can somehow save ourselves (see 13:18).

John pictures both idolatry and the punishment for idolatry with wine. Those who were led astray by the "maddening wine" (verse 8) of false teachings on earth will now be forced to drink "the wine of God's fury" (verse 10). The wine of God's fury is his anger against those who refused Jesus and sought to save themselves by some other means. This wine will be poured "full strength" on the day of judgment (verse 10). God's anger against unbelief shows itself already in this life (see 9:20). Sinners go through this life with accusing consciences, they suffer the consequences of their sins, and they reel under the warning judgments God sends to lead them to repentance. But none of that trouble matches the undiluted display of God's anger in eternity.

Eternal death is the "cup of his wrath" (verse 10). This cup is the instrument from which God serves the idolater the bitter wine of his fury. "He will be tormented with burning sulfur" (verse 10; see 19:20; 21:8). The burning sulfur reminds us of the way God destroyed Sodom and Gomorrah. Jude writes, "Sodom and Gomorrah and the surrounding towns gave themselves up to sexual immorality and perversion.

They serve as an example of those who suffer the punishment of eternal fire" (Jude 7).

The Bible regularly describes hell as a fire. Jesus said that anger puts us "in danger of the fire of hell" (Matthew 5:22). The writer to the Hebrews describes hell as a "raging fire that will consume the enemies of God" (Hebrews 10:27). The anguish of the damned will be intensified because they will suffer "in the presence of the holy angels and of the Lamb" (verse 10). As "those who pierced him" (1:7) will have to face the Savior at the judgment, so those who fought against the Lamb and his holy angels will suffer in their presence.

The last judgment is final. There is no second chance, no opportunity for the enemies of the church to repent. "The smoke of their torment rises for ever and ever. There is no rest day or night for those who worship the beast" (verse 11). Jesus called hell "eternal fire" (Matthew 18:8) and said it is a place "where the fire never goes out" (Mark 9:43). At the judgment Jesus will say to his enemies, "Depart from me, you who are cursed, into the eternal fire prepared for the devil and his angels" (Matthew 25:41).

Those who deny the existence of hell speak against Scripture. Those who say that hell is annihilation, not eternal punishment, ignore John's record of the third angel's words. The saying "Where there's smoke, there's fire" helps explain the angel's threat: "The smoke of their torment rises for ever and ever" (verse 11). The fires of hell that cause torment are never extinguished.

"This calls for patient endurance on the part of the saints who obey God's commandments and remain faithful to Jesus" (verse 12). John's encouragement to believers comes at the end of the three angels' messages. The saints must contemplate all they have heard in this vision. Remain faithful to Jesus, he says. Hold on to the eternal gospel. With patient endurance bear the hardships of the last days, trusting that God has already declared Babylon's destruction. Obey God's commandments and refuse to be marked by the image of the beast.

The voice that John heard "from heaven" (verse 13) is the voice of Jesus that first commissioned him to write (1:19). For the sake of the patient, suffering saints, Jesus offers another view of the glory of the saints in eternity: "Blessed are the dead who die in the Lord from now on" (verse 13). Appropriately, these words comfort mourners at every Lutheran burial service. Those who die in faith are forever blessed. Blessedness is spiritual happiness. Jesus promised that those who hear the word of God and obey it will be blessed (Luke 11:28). The taste of blessedness we receive through the promises of the gospel on earth results in the perfect happiness of eternity. Revelation provides fuller descriptions of this blessedness in chapters 7, 21, and 22.

The Holy Spirit confirms Jesus' promise of heaven. Jesus once said, "The Holy Spirit . . . will remind you of everything I have said to you" (John 14:26). The Spirit says heaven is a rest. The Old Testament Sabbath provided God's people a day of rest once a week. But the Sabbath foreshadowed a greater rest, one that only Jesus can provide. "There remains, then, a Sabbath-rest for the people of God; for anyone who enters God's rest also rests from his own work, just as God did from his" (Hebrews 4:9,10). This rest, however, should not be confused with the boredom and inactivity that many cynics have ascribed to heaven. Heavenly rest is an end to the labor of this life that is constantly embittered by sin. Heavenly rest involves service, ruling (22:3-5), and joyful singing (see 14:2,3).

The deeds of the saints "will follow them" (verse 13). This does not mean that God will judge us worthy of heaven on the basis of what we have done. This may mean that, even after we die, our good works follow us on earth as a testimony to our faith. The more likely meaning, however, is that our good works follow us to the day of judgment when God cites them as evidence that we believed in Jesus for our salvation. This is the sense in which Jesus recounted the good works of the righteous in his parable of the sheep and the goats (Matthew 25:31-46).

The sixth vision: the harvest

¹⁴I looked, and there before me was a white cloud, and seated on the cloud was one "like a son of man" with a crown of gold on his head and a sharp sickle in his hand. ¹⁵Then another angel came out of the temple and called in a loud voice to him who was sitting on the cloud, "Take your sickle and reap, because the time to reap has come, for the harvest of the earth is ripe." ¹⁶So he who was seated on the cloud swung his sickle over the earth, and the earth was harvested.

¹⁷Another angel came out of the temple in heaven, and he too had a sharp sickle. ¹⁸Still another angel, who had charge of the fire, came from the altar and called in a loud voice to him who had the sharp sickle, "Take your sharp sickle and gather the clusters of grapes from the earth's vine, because its grapes are ripe." ¹⁹The angel swung his sickle on the earth, gathered its grapes and threw them into the great winepress of God's wrath. ²⁰They were trampled in the winepress outside the city, and blood flowed out of the press, rising as high as the horses' bridles for a distance of 1,600 stadia.

The vision of the harvest is the sixth of the seven visions. John saw Jesus seated on a white cloud with a sharp sickle in this hand. Like so many of the visions, the harvest comforts the saints while it causes dread in the hearts of the unrepentant. Believers look forward to their Savior's return. Jesus told us, "At that time they will see the Son of Man coming in a cloud with power and great glory. When these things begin to take place, stand up and lift up your heads, because your redemption is drawing near" (Luke 21:27,28).

At the Last Day we will be judged by a peer, by someone who is like us. John emphasizes Jesus' human nature when he writes that the one he saw on the white cloud was "one 'like a son of man.'" Paul made the same point: "For he has set a day when he will judge the world with justice by the man he has appointed. He has given proof of this to all men by raising him from the dead" (Acts 17:31). The crown of gold on his head is not the pretentious diadem worn by the dragon (see 12:3) and the beast (see 13:1). His is the crown of victory that he shares with his fellow victors, the saints (see 4:4).

Jesus will come to harvest the earth with a "sickle in his hand" (verse 14). The "sharp" sickle (verse 14) will not miss a single stalk. "Every eye will see him" (1:7). In the verses that follow, three angels assist Jesus in the final harvest. The number 3 indicates that they are all agents of God. They came "out of the temple" (verses 15,17) and "from the altar" (verse 18) in heaven. Jesus had said that he would return "in his Father's glory with his holy angels" (Mark 8:38). In the parable of the weeds he explained that the "harvest is the end of the age, and the harvesters are the angels" (Matthew 13:39). The first and second angels assist Jesus in the harvest of the righteous.

In a loud voice, the first of these two angels heralds this important announcement: "The time to reap has come" (verse 15). As in the rest of Scripture, the imminent return of Jesus and the final judgment is a recurring theme in Revelation. John the Baptist announced Jesus' first coming in anticipation of his final harvest: "His winnowing fork is in his hand, and he will clear his threshing floor, gathering his wheat into the barn and burning up the chaff with unquenchable fire"

(Matthew 3:12). Time for repentance runs out. The time for Jesus' return will come soon. All seven visions in Revelation reflect this urgent tone. The Lord's last words to John at the end of this book endorse this theme: "Yes, I am coming soon" (22:20).

A third angel "had charge of the fire" (verse 18). He is God's agent for punishing the damned. This angel resembles the angel with the golden censer who stood at the altar (see 8:3-5). That angel filled the censer with fire from the altar. That fire signified the judgments God brings on the unrepentant before the final judgment. By contrast, this third angel has charge of the fire of hell.

John's mention of the sickle, grapes, and the winepress in connection with this angel makes this part of the vision consistent with a prophecy of Joel. Joel wrote, "Swing the sickle, for the harvest is ripe. Come, trample the grapes, for the winepress is full and the vats overflow—so great is their wickedness!" (Joel 3:13). The grapes are the wicked. The fact that the "grapes are ripe" (verse 18) means that their wickedness has matured to the limit God set for it. John explains that the winepress is "God's wrath" (verse 19; see 14:10).

The horrifying picture of eternal punishment in verse 20 attests to the absolute holiness of God. God overlooks no sin. If sin goes unrepented and unforgiven, God must punish it. To complete his picture of harvesting grapes, John says that the unbelievers "were trampled in the winepress outside the city" (verse 20; see 11:2). The holy city, Jerusalem, is a symbol of the presence of God and the dwelling of his people. Old Testament writers used a burning dumpsite outside the holy city as a synonym for hell. When Jesus was crucified outside the city, he cried out in anguish that God had forsaken him. The unholy will be punished away from the presence of the holy God.

VISION OF THE SEVEN BOWLS OF WRATH CONTAINING THE SEVEN LAST PLAGUES (15:1–16:21)

The seventh vision: the seven angels with the seven plagues

15 I saw in heaven another great and marvelous sign: seven angels with the seven last plagues—last, because with them God's wrath is completed. ²And I saw what looked like a sea of glass mixed with fire and, standing beside the sea, those who had been victorious over the beast and his image and over the number of his name. They held harps given them by God ³and sang the song of Moses the servant of God and the song of the Lamb:

"Great and marvelous are your deeds,
    Lord God Almighty.
Just and true are your ways,
    King of the ages.
⁴Who will not fear you, O Lord,
    and bring glory to your name?
For you alone are holy.
All nations will come
    and worship before you,
for your righteous acts have been revealed."

⁵After this I looked and in heaven the temple, that is, the tabernacle of the Testimony, was opened. ⁶Out of the temple came the seven angels with the seven plagues. They were dressed in clean, shining linen and wore golden sashes around their chests. ⁷Then one of the four living creatures gave to the seven angels seven golden bowls filled with the wrath of God, who lives for ever and ever. ⁸And the temple was filled with smoke from the glory of God and from his power, and no one could enter the temple until the seven plagues of the seven angels were completed.

"All nations will come and worship before you." (15:4)

Just as the last trumpet of the third vision introduced the fourth, so the last vision in the vision of the seven visions introduces the fifth, the vision of the plagues. In chapter 15 John sees "seven angels with the seven last plagues" (verse 1). In chapter 16 these angels "pour out the seven bowls of God's wrath on the earth" (16:1).

As we move from the end of the fourth vision to the beginning of the fifth, we move back again in time. The fourth vision ended with the final harvest and eternal punishment. The fifth vision takes us back to the New Testament age before the judgment. The plagues of the seven angels are called the "last, because with them God's wrath is completed" (verse 1). That means they lead up to the final judgment.

In heaven John saw "what looked like a sea of glass" (verse 2). This is the same sea of glass that he had seen before (see 4:6). As with the first sea, however, this one also cannot be precisely interpreted. It may be a picture of peace and serenity in the presence of God. Unlike the first sea, however, this one is mixed with fire. Fire hints at anger and judgment. After John saw the first sea, his vision continued with pictures of the peace of heaven and the glory of God. Soon after John sees this sea, Jesus reveals God's judgment on the wicked. The fire that mixed with the glassy sea may be a reflection of God's impending anger.

Standing next to the sea are the saints in glory. They were faithful unto death and "had been victorious over the beast" (verse 2; see 13:16-18). Earlier, John said the choir of the saints sounded like harpists playing their harps (14:2). Now the saints are holding harps that God gave them and are singing. The song they are singing is a song of victory (verse 3). Their victory song is much like Moses' song of victory at the Red Sea (Exodus 15:1-18).

The song of the saints gives all glory to God for the victory. In that sense it is also "the song of the Lamb" (verse 3). As God won his victory at the Red Sea through his servant Moses, so he won the victory over the beast through his servant Jesus, the Lamb. The victors in heaven praise God because he is powerful, the "Lord God Almighty," fair and "just," eternal, the "King of the ages," and "holy" (verse 4).

When the song of the saints ended, John saw seven angels with seven plagues come out of the tabernacle of the Testimony (verses 5,6). This is another picture of God's presence drawn from the Old Testament. Until now, Solomon's temple in Jerusalem symbolized God's presence in John's visions. Now, however, John sees the tabernacle, the movable tent-church that Moses constructed for God's people in the wilderness.

The angels' white linen clothing designates them as servants of the holy God, and their golden sashes show they are royal agents of the King. Once the angels were outside the tabernacle, one of the four living creatures gave them seven bowls filled with God's wrath (verse 7). The four living creatures symbolize the whole created world (see 4:6-9). In the next chapter, all the bowls of God's wrath affect the created world.

The temple was filled with smoke in John's vision (verse 8) just as it was in Isaiah's (Isaiah 6:4). John explains that the smoke came "from the glory of God and from his power" (verse 8). God's glory is his loving faithfulness to his promises. He may exercise that faithfulness by saving and protecting his people or by judging and punishing their enemies. The fiery reflection in the sea of glass (see verse 2) may have been a hint that the glory and power of God are about to carry out his wrath on his enemies. God's judgment has been determined. No one is allowed to enter the temple to intercede and ask him to relent.

The first five bowls

16 Then I heard a loud voice from the temple saying to the seven angels, "Go, pour out the seven bowls of God's wrath on the earth."

[2]The first angel went and poured out his bowl on the land, and ugly and painful sores broke out on the people who had the mark of the beast and worshiped his image.

[3]The second angel poured out his bowl on the sea, and it turned into blood like that of a dead man, and every living thing in the sea died.

[4]The third angel poured out his bowl on the rivers and springs of water, and they became blood. [5]Then I heard the angel in charge of the waters say:

"You are just in these judgments,
 you who are and who were, the Holy One,
 because you have so judged;
[6] for they have shed the blood of your saints and prophets,
 and you have given them blood to drink
 as they deserve."

[7]And I heard the altar respond:

"Yes, Lord God Almighty,
 true and just are your judgments."

[8]The fourth angel poured out his bowl on the sun, and the sun was given power to scorch people with fire. [9]They were seared by the intense heat and they cursed the name of God, who had control over these plagues, but they refused to repent and glorify him.

[10]The fifth angel poured out his bowl on the throne of the beast, and his kingdom was plunged into darkness. Men gnawed their tongues in agony [11]and cursed the God of heaven

because of their pains and their sores, but they refused to repent of what they had done.

The seven angels introduced in the last chapter are now sent out on their mission: "Go, pour out the seven bowls of God's wrath on the earth" (verse 1). A voice from the temple sends them to empty their bowls. Later, this voice is identified as the voice of God "from the throne" (verse 17). Although many of the signs of the Last Day seem like natural disasters, they are all sent by the will of God.

The seven bowls of wrath share many similarities with the seven trumpets in the third vision (8:6–9:21). The first four bowls of wrath, like the first four trumpets, predict natural disasters that lead up to the day of judgment. These four bowls also recall some of the plagues on Egypt that God announced through Moses (Exodus 7–11).

The first angel poured his bowl on the land (verse 2). Those who worshiped the beast (see 13:16-18) were afflicted with painful sores. These may symbolize the natural consequences of sin that the wicked suffer. The beast represents the devil's influence through world government and the false teaching of self-help religions. These painful sores are the disappointment and frustration that come to the wicked when their misplaced trust in human saviors betrays them.

The second angel poured his bowl of God's wrath on the sea (verse 3). The third poured his bowl on the inland waterways (verse 4). In both cases the water turned to blood. Environmental disasters should not be read as judgments only on those who mismanage the earth. The deterioration of the earth's vital resources (like water) reminds all the wicked of the destructive nature of sin. "For the creation was subjected to frustration, not by its own choice, but by the will of the one who subjected it" (Romans 8:20). Gradual and sudden

155

declines in the earth's environment are not merely natural phenomena. They are purposeful reminders of God's wrath against a world headed for final judgment.

The angel in charge of the waters is the one God appointed to pour out his wrath on the inland waters. Water is vital to all life on earth. In the wake of terrible natural destruction, this agent of God defends God's justice in carrying out this judgment. "You are just in these judgments," he says (verse 5). God always was and always will be "the Holy One" (verse 5). If we try to judge God by individual disasters he allows, we will never understand his justice. We must always look at God's fairness in the context of his eternal plans. Every trouble he allows in the natural world is sent to strengthen the faith of his saints and draw the wicked to repentance. God dispenses justice in kind. The bloody waters are a fitting judgment for those who "have shed the blood of your saints and prophets" (verse 6). For those who refuse the forgiveness God offers in the gospel, there remains only the "life for life" justice of his holy law (Deuteronomy 19:21).

The altar responded to confirm the angel's praise of God's fairness (verse 7). The altar is the place from which God's punitive justice proceeds. In the vision of the seven trumpets, the angel filled the censer with fire from the altar and hurled it on the earth (8:5). In the vision of the seven visions, the angel in charge of the fire came from the altar (14:18). John says he heard "the altar respond" (verse 7). We understand this to mean the voice of the angel who came from the altar. He is God's agent to carry out justice against the wicked.

"The fourth angel poured out his bowl on the sun" (verse 8). The sun was not darkened as it was in the fourth trumpet (8:12) but intensified. People on earth "were seared by the intense heat" (verse 9). In Jesus' prophecies of the last days, Matthew and Mark record that the sun will be darkened. But Luke records our Lord's general prediction about disturbances in the heavens: "There will be signs in the sun, moon and stars. . . . the heavenly bodies will be shaken" (Luke 21:25,26). Any disturbance in the earth's heat source has terrible consequences for all life on the planet.

Despite the terror that natural disaster causes, God in love uses these judgments to shake the wicked from their complacency. The nearer we get to the end, however, the more God's display of wrath will harden sinners, and fewer will repent. John writes, "They cursed the name of God, who had control over these plagues" (verse 9). Hardened sinners are forced to acknowledge that God's will stands behind natural disasters. Set on saving themselves, they refuse to repent and glorify God for his salvation. Yet they curse the name of God. God's name is his reputation for redeeming sinners through the blood of the Lamb.

The angel with the fifth trumpet brought anguish for "those people who did not have the seal of God on their foreheads" (see 9:4). The fifth bowl brings judgment on the same people. Two beasts are mentioned in chapter 13, but here John describes what happened to the "throne" and the "kingdom" of one of the beasts. That suggests that the first beast, world governments manipulated by Satan, is meant here. "His kingdom was plunged into darkness" (verse 10) means that, in the end, world governments will fail to deliver those things for which people worshiped them. It will become apparent to all that they cannot bring social justice, world peace, or heaven on earth.

Those who trusted in themselves, "Mother Earth," and world government to bring them happiness have seen their idols deposed by the first five bowls. Their anguish is piling

157

up. They suffer "painful sores" (verse 2), the personal consequences of sin. Their physical world has been racked by natural disasters. Their secular, satanic rulers have proved ineffective. Still, stubborn in their unbelief, "they refused to repent of what they had done" (verse 11). In all these troubles they see God's hand of "control" (verse 9), but they refuse the forgiveness he extends in the name of the Lamb.

The sixth bowl: the battle of Armageddon

[12]The sixth angel poured out his bowl on the great river Euphrates, and its water was dried up to prepare the way for the kings from the East. [13]Then I saw three evil spirits that looked like frogs; they came out of the mouth of the dragon, out of the mouth of the beast and out of the mouth of the false prophet. [14]They are spirits of demons performing miraculous signs, and they go out to the kings of the whole world, to gather them for the battle on the great day of God Almighty.

[15]"Behold, I come like a thief! Blessed is he who stays awake and keeps his clothes with him, so that he may not go naked and be shamefully exposed."

[16]Then they gathered the kings together to the place that in Hebrew is called Armageddon.

The sixth and seventh bowls of wrath depict the New Testament age immediately before the final judgment. The hearts of the wicked are firmly hardened. No mention of repentance comes after the fifth bowl. Only God's elect remain faithful. "Because of the increase of wickedness, the love of most will grow cold" (Matthew 24:12).

The parallels between the visions of the trumpets and the bowls continue. At the sound of the sixth trumpet, "the four angels who are bound at the great river Euphrates" (9:14) were released. Now "the sixth angel poured out his bowl on the great river Euphrates" (verse 12). The kingdoms in the

Euphrates river area were the great enemies of Israel in the Old Testament. In John's vision the Euphrates river stands for all the great enemies of the New Testament church.

This unholy alliance is described. John saw "three evil spirits" (verse 13). They had the appearance of frogs because they arose from the Euphrates. One of these evil spirits came out of the mouth of the dragon, or Satan (12:9). The second came out of the mouth of the beast, the first beast in chapter 13. This beast is described here as the alliance of the kings from the East and "the kings of the whole world" (verse 14). All world governments increasingly will be in service to Satan.

The third evil spirit comes out of the mouth of the false prophet, the second beast of chapter 13. He preaches salvation by man—man's works, man's world, man's government. The interrelationship of the pictures in John's vision makes an important point. The enemies of the church may take many forms, but they have one source. The two beasts in chapter 13 are both allies of Satan. Satan, the beast, and the false prophet all work together in this vision. The lies that the three evil spirits tell and the deceptive miracles they perform all share Satan's purpose of destroying the church. They all aim "to gather" the enemies of God "for the battle on the great day of God Almighty" (verse 14).

Jesus interjects a brief word of warning into John's description of the sixth bowl. "Behold, I come like a thief!" he says (verse 15). Even though he is not introduced, we know this is Jesus speaking. He has spoken this way before (Matthew 24:43), and he will speak this way again (Revelation 22:12). Both Paul and Peter write that "the day of the Lord will come like a thief" (1 Thessalonians 5:2; 2 Peter 3:10). Jesus' interjection is not an invitation to the wicked to repent on that day. His words are addressed to John's readers throughout the New Testament age.

The Lord appeals to us to stay "awake" spiritually (verse 15). This is a plea to avoid Satan's temptations that come in so many deceiving forms. "Watch and pray so that you will not fall into temptation," Jesus told his sleeping disciples at Gethsemane (Matthew 26:41). Spiritual watchfulness wards off lost faith. Jesus compares holding on to faith with keeping your clothes with you. Our "clothes" are the white robes of Jesus' righteousness that he gives the saints to wear (see 3:4-6; 18). Only his righteousness can keep the nakedness of our sin from being shamefully exposed at the judgment predicted by this bowl.

John returns to his description of the sixth bowl. The three evil spirits gather the kings of the world together at Armageddon. Millenialists have tried in vain to assign specific dates and political powers to this Bible verse. They have regularly been embarrassed when the predicted end times elapse without event. We must remember that John has been speaking figuratively throughout this vision. We associate Armageddon with Mount Carmel on the plain north of Jerusalem where Elijah defeated the followers of the pagan god Baal (1 Kings 18:19-40). From this it is clear that Armageddon is not a place or time in history for some military confrontation between believers and their enemies. Rather, Armageddon symbolizes the stubborn, united resistance with which God's enemies face him at the final judgment. Now follows the bowl that envisions that day.

The seventh bowl: the end of the world

¹⁷**The seventh angel poured out his bowl into the air, and out of the temple came a loud voice from the throne, saying, "It is done!" ¹⁸Then there came flashes of lightning, rumblings, peals**

of thunder and a severe earthquake. No earthquake like it has ever occurred since man has been on earth, so tremendous was the quake. ¹⁹The great city split into three parts, and the cities of the nations collapsed. God remembered Babylon the Great and gave her the cup filled with the wine of the fury of his wrath. ²⁰Every island fled away and the mountains could not be found. ²¹From the sky huge hailstones of about a hundred pounds each fell upon men. And they cursed God on account of the plague of hail, because the plague was so terrible.

The loud voice of God "from the throne" (verse 17) confirms that this vision pictures the Last Day, the day of judgment. "It is done!" God says (verse 17). With this seventh bowl, all the bowls of his wrath have been poured out. God's patience has run out. All his drastic attempts to bring the wicked to repentance are expired. This bowl is not poured out on the land, the sea, the inland waters, the sun, the thrones of earthly power, or the seat of God's enemies. It is poured out into the air. This display of God's wrath includes everybody and everything under the heavens.

Many writers see the events in verses 17 to 21 as taking place some time before the Last Day. To them the verses describe a series of events that end while the wicked are still cursing God (verse 21). After God announces that his wrath is completed, however, John gives no hint of the passing of time. All these verses together picture the quick destruction of the earth. Peter writes, "The day of the Lord will come like a thief. The heavens will disappear with a roar; the elements will be destroyed by fire, and the earth and everything in it will be laid bare" (2 Peter 3:10). All these things take place on that one, final day.

As on Mount Sinai, thunder and lightning appear in Revelation as signs of God's holiness. The "severe earthquake" (verse 18; 11:13) is not like the many other earthquakes

(Matthew 24:7) that warn of judgment day. No earthquake like this one ever has occurred before. It is one of the destructive forces God uses to bring an end to the world on the Last Day. The earthquake causes the city to split into three parts (verse 19). The great city is the holy city. Here, as in chapter 11, Jerusalem is where the church carries on its struggle against its enemies. The number 3 is the number of God. He will destroy Jerusalem and all the cities on earth on the Last Day.

"God remembered Babylon the Great" (verse 19), that is, he remembered all the false teaching and idolatry the enemies of his church perpetrated (see 14:8). These words describe judgment day, not the end times before the judgment. Leaving the image of the bowls of wrath, John returns to the "cup filled with the wine of the fury of his wrath" (verse 19). This is the picture the third angel used to describe the final punishment of those who worship the beast (14:9,10). The church's enemies will be forced to drink God's anger to the fullest. This is not a warning to repent. It is a prophecy of eternal punishment—torment "with burning sulfur in the presence of the holy angels and of the Lamb" (14:10).

The complete destruction of the world accompanies the final destruction of the church's enemies. "Every island fled away and the mountains could not be found" (verse 20). The earth as we know it will be gone. The horror of this final destruction will appear as huge hailstones to the unbeliever. Ezekiel also pictured God's destructive anger as hailstones (Ezekiel 13:11,13). The natural response of those without hope in the judgment is to curse God. But on that same day they will be forced to give unwilling "glory to the God of heaven" (11:13). Then every knee will bow at the name of Jesus "in heaven and on earth and under the earth" (Philippians 2:10).

"Since everything will be destroyed in this way, what kind of people ought you to be? You ought to live holy and godly lives as you look forward to the day of God and speed its coming. That day will bring about the destruction of the heavens by fire, and the elements will melt in the heat. But in keeping with his promise we are looking forward to a new heaven and a new earth, the home of righteousness" (2 Peter 3:11-13).

VISION OF CHRIST AND ANTICHRIST
(17:1–19:21)

The great harlot

17 One of the seven angels who had the seven bowls came and said to me, "Come, I will show you the punishment of the great prostitute, who sits on many waters. ²With her the kings of the earth committed adultery and the inhabitants of the earth were intoxicated with the wine of her adulteries."

³Then the angel carried me away in the Spirit into a desert. There I saw a woman sitting on a scarlet beast that was covered with blasphemous names and had seven heads and ten horns. ⁴The woman was dressed in purple and scarlet, and was glittering with gold, precious stones and pearls. She held a golden cup in her hand, filled with abominable things and the filth of her adulteries. ⁵This title was written on her forehead:

MYSTERY

BABYLON THE GREAT

THE MOTHER OF PROSTITUTES

AND OF THE ABOMINATIONS OF THE EARTH.

⁶I saw that the woman was drunk with the blood of the saints, the blood of those who bore testimony to Jesus.

When I saw her, I was greatly astonished. ⁷Then the angel said to me: "Why are you astonished? I will explain to you the mystery of the woman and of the beast she rides, which has the seven heads and ten horns. ⁸The beast, which you saw, once was, now is not, and will come up out of the Abyss and go to his destruction. The inhabitants of the earth whose names have not been written in the book of life from the creation of the world will be astonished when they see the beast, because he once was, now is not, and yet will come.

⁹"This calls for a mind with wisdom. The seven heads are seven hills on which the woman sits. They are also seven kings. ¹⁰Five have fallen, one is, the other has not yet come; but when he does come, he must remain for a little while. ¹¹The beast who once was, and now is not, is an eighth king. He belongs to the seven and is going to his destruction.

¹²"The ten horns you saw are ten kings who have not yet received a kingdom, but who for one hour will receive authority as kings along with the beast. ¹³They have one purpose and will give their power and authority to the beast. ¹⁴They will make war against the Lamb, but the Lamb will overcome them because he is Lord of lords and King of kings—and with him will be his called, chosen and faithful followers."

¹⁵Then the angel said to me, "The waters you saw, where the prostitute sits, are people, multitudes, nations and languages. ¹⁶The beast and the ten horns you saw will hate the prostitute. They will bring her to ruin and leave her naked; they will eat her flesh and burn her with fire. ¹⁷For God has put it into their hearts to accomplish his purpose by agreeing to give the beast their power to rule, until God's words are fulfilled. ¹⁸The woman you saw is the great city that rules over the kings of the earth."

One of the angels from the vision of the bowls introduces John to the next vision, the vision of Christ and antichrist. This is the sixth vision of the Revelation. Although it describes many troubles for the church, the angel reveals Jesus' loving purpose in offering this vision. "I will show you the punishment of the great prostitute," he says (verse 1). In the face of the fiercest opposition, Jesus wants the church to know that he has guaranteed victory over its enemies.

Chapter 17 identifies the great prostitute, chapter 18 predicts her downfall and destruction, and chapter 19 glimpses the victory song the saints will sing after Christ's victory.

The great prostitute sits on many waters (verse 1). The angel explains the waters in verse 15: "The waters you saw, where the prostitute sits, are peoples, multitudes, nations and languages." "The prostitute sits" means that she sits in a position of authority to influence people all over the world. "The inhabitants of the earth were intoxicated with the wine of her adulteries" (verse 2). Earlier, John said that Babylon "made all the nations drink the maddening wine of her adulteries" (14:8). This adultery is not sexual sin but spiritual unfaithfulness (see 14:8). Most of the people on earth will be taken up with—"intoxicated" with—the teachings of this unfaithful church.

With this prostitute "the kings of the earth committed adultery" (verse 2). This is the same unholy alliance of the two beasts in chapter 13. The prostitute is the false church that preaches salvation through human achievement. Since salvation by works is man's natural religion, secular governments find easy partnership with this prostitute. Throughout the New Testament age, churches that emphasize legal obedience for salvation have found it easy to mix church and state. But churches commit adultery against Christ when they go to bed with government.

In order to paint a more detailed picture of this prostitute, the angel carried John away "into a desert" (verse 3). This is figurative language. John was not physically carried to a desert by the Holy Spirit. He was carried "in spirit" (see 1:10; 4:2) to envision a desert. There he saw "a woman sitting on a scarlet beast" (verse 3). In an earlier vision the woman in the desert (12:6,14) was Jesus' true church. The woman in this vision bears some resemblance to that first one. Both are women. Both are in the desert, that is, the world of the New Testament age. Both outwardly profess attachment to Christ. In some aspects, the false church will always resemble the true and faithful church.

It soon becomes clear, however, that the woman in this vision is not the true church. She was "sitting on a scarlet beast that was covered with blasphemous names and had seven heads and ten horns" (verse 3). Scarlet is the color of royalty. The beast is marked with seven heads and ten horns, the same as the beast from the sea in chapter 13. This woman is in a ruling position on the beast. This is another picture of the ungodly church and state partnership that promotes salvation by works. The blasphemous names covering the beast show that it does not give glory to God's grace in Jesus.

The false, unfaithful church is a rich church. The woman was "glittering with gold, precious stones and pearls. She held a golden cup in her hand, filled with abominable things and the filth of her adulteries" (verse 4). At Laodicea affluence led to indifference and false doctrine (3:14-18). The opposite is pictured here. The prostitute grew affluent through her false teachings and influential relationships with worldly powers. She displays her brazen attitude by wearing her name on her forehead. She claims to be married to Christ but by her false teaching sells herself to worldly philosophies.

False teaching is always served in a golden cup. Christ crucified is a "stumbling block" and "foolishness" (1 Corinthians 1:23). Social gospel, on the other hand, makes golden promises of a better life in this world. Teaching self-image and touting human accomplishment allows the false church to sit with the rich without embarrassment. Yet drinking from this golden cup poisons her relationship to Christ. Those who hold to the cross recognize with John that the teachings of the false church are "abominable things" (verse 4) that involve us in the filth of the false church's "adulteries" (verse 4).

On her forehead, a prominent place, the woman identifies herself as "Babylon the Great" (verse 5). John has already identified Babylon as the great enemy of Christ's church and predicted its destruction (14:8). Her open liaison with secular powers brands her a prostitute. In fact, she is "the mother of prostitutes" (verse 5), worse than a prostitute. Not satisfied to betray Christ herself, she spawns and trains others to be unfaithful to their Savior. She should be regarded as what her actions advertise her to be: mother of "the abominations of the earth" (verse 5). She should be a most detestable, repulsive figure to those looking for salvation.

The "Mystery" is that she is not regarded as such. Her open lies make her all the more deceitful. The false church mentions Jesus but emphasizes what man must do to put himself into the good graces of God. When Paul warned about the man of lawlessness in 2 Thessalonians 2:7, he used the same Greek word for mystery. There the NIV translated it as "secret power." "God sends them a powerful delusion, so that they will believe the lie" (2 Thessalonians 2:11). Yet the mystery will be unraveled. In spite of his deceit, Paul writes, the man of lawlessness will be revealed for what he really is. Jesus will overthrow him "with the breath of his mouth" (2 Thessalonians 2:8). As this vision proceeds, we will see that this prostitute also will be revealed and destroyed.

John "saw that the woman was drunk with the blood of the saints" (verse 6). John wrote to persecuted Christians. He asked the congregation in Smyrna to be faithful, "even to the point of death" (2:10). His first readers knew the false church was not content to destroy souls. In league with satanic secular powers, it seeks the death of the saints. In our marriage vows we promise faithfulness until death parts us. Not even death, however, can separate the church, the bride of Christ, from her beloved.

John himself knew what persecution was. He wrote Revelation from exile. The prostitute and the beast marked John for exile "because of the word of God and the testimony of Jesus"

(1:9). In the same way, in this vision the woman was able to recognize the saints and mark them for bloodshed because they "bore testimony to Jesus" (verse 6). Still today, those who seek righteousness through their own works are able to identify those who are righteous through faith in Christ. Throughout their lives, the latter bear testimony to Jesus.

John was horrified at the terrible vision of the prostitute. When the angel saw this, he began to explain the mystery of the woman and the beast to John (verse 7). Earlier, the four living creatures described God as the One "who was, and is, and is to come" (4:8). The angel describes the beast as the one who "once was, now is not, and will come up out of the Abyss" (verse 8). The beast with seven heads pretends to be like God but is not. Unlike the changeless, eternal God, the beast will appear, disappear, and then appear again. In the end God will destroy him.

Those "whose names have not been written in the book of life" (verse 8) will be taken in by the godlike pretensions of the beast. Each time the beast appears on the stage of history, most of the world will marvel at his resiliency. Although Scripture and history prove that he will be destroyed, people will be impressed by his power. The beast represents secular power under the control of Satan. He is identical to the beast from the sea (see 13:1-8). He is teamed with the prostitute, the false church. Believers may expect this devilish duo to arise again and again to harm the true church.

Identifying the woman "calls for a mind with wisdom" (verse 9). John also called for wisdom at the end of chapter 13 (verse 18). The false church, represented by the woman here, was there pictured as the beast out of the earth. Jesus' visions repeatedly describe and identify this great enemy of the church because her deceit characterizes the spiritual condition of the last days. To remain faithful to Jesus, God's people must be able to recognize her. Jesus warns us, "Watch out that no one deceives you. For many will come in my name, claiming, 'I am the Christ,' and will deceive many" (Matthew 24:4,5).

After calling for wisdom, the angel completes his description of the prostitute and the beast. In chapter 13, verse 1, and again in verse 3 of this chapter, the beast is described as having seven heads. Now the angel explains that "the seven heads are seven hills on which the woman sits" (verse 9).

Some understand the beast to correspond literally to the seven hills of Jerusalem. Jerusalem was the seat of the Sanhedrin. On this ruling body sat the self-righteous Jewish leaders who harassed Jesus' ministry and were instrumental in his death. Jerusalem was also the home base for the Judaizers who persecuted the Christian congregations in Asia Minor with their demands for the new Gentile Christians to be circumcised and obey the Old Testament ceremonies.

The city of Rome also sat on seven hills. Many writers are convinced that John is describing the Roman government, which was active in persecuting believers at the time Revelation was written. Some of the Roman caesars demanded to be worshiped as gods, and they put to death Christians who would not bow to them. Later, the Roman church became an ally of the government in Rome. To this day the papacy maintains its seat of authority in Rome. This unholy alliance of church and state is responsible for centuries of false doctrine, mixing the teaching of Christ with demands for human accomplishments. At times, Rome physically persecuted those "who bore testimony to Jesus" (verse 6), burning John Huss and John Wycliff at the stake and slaying the Huguenots, for example.

No doubt Jerusalem and Rome are indicated by the seven-headed beast. But the number 7 is used figuratively in Revelation. It either stands for God's gracious work among the people on earth, or it represents those who pretend to be doing God's work (see 12:3). Here 7 symbolizes all secular governments that claim divine rights and ally themselves with the false church. Jerusalem and Rome are prominent examples, but they do not exhaust the symbolism of the seven hills.

What is true of the seven hills is also true of the seven kings. The seven kings represent the same thing as the seven hills, that is, secular government's alliance with the false church. The number 7 does not point to seven specific kings or kingdoms. It highlights the deceptive way world governments make claims to divine power and rights. John writes that five of these kings have fallen (verse 10). The number 10 signifies a limit set by God (see 2:10; 12:3). The number 5 is half that limit. Accordingly, the five kings who have fallen represent the five world powers that had fallen in Old Testament times and the restrictions God places on oppressive world powers in the New Testament.

The numbers assigned to the kings in this vision do not represent specific world powers but describe the general *nature* of all of them. The seven heads and the ten horns all belong to the beast ridden by the prostitute. All world governments under the influence of Satan, in the Old and New Testaments, share the same characteristics. They all "have one purpose and will give their power and authority to the beast" (verse 13). They aid and abet the false church and lay claim to divine right. But they are limited by God. They will appear and then disappear from history.

The two kings who follow the first five share these characteristics. One is in power now (verse 10), but, like the beast, sometime soon it will be said of him that he "now is not" (verse 8). Then the seventh king will appear but will remain

171

for only "a little while" (verse 10). He is like the beast himself who comes and goes from world prominence and "belongs to the seven" (verse 11).

When John received this vision, ten kings "have not yet received a kingdom" (verse 12). These are governments that serve the beast in the New Testament age. The number 10 does not point to specific world powers during the last two thousand years. Rather, it assures believers that God limits the time these governments will stay in power. He keeps a tight rein on their efforts to harm the saints (see verse 17). God will allow them to exercise their authority for only "one hour" (verse 12).

Surrounded by every outward evidence to the contrary, believers in every age can trust that their Savior is in control of the events of history. "He is Lord of lords and King of kings" (verse 14). Even while the beast is making "war against the Lamb" (verse 14), we know "the Lamb will overcome" (verse 14). Jesus purchased our eternal glory through humiliation and suffering. He will stay with us through our earthly troubles and deliver us to that glory. "Rejoice that you participate in the sufferings of Christ, so that you may be overjoyed when his glory is revealed" (1 Peter 4:13). Faith is the evidence of things not seen. Amid the short-lived triumphs of the beast and the prostitute, we look to Jesus' final victory. When he returns, "with him will be his called, chosen and faithful followers" (verse 14).

Already before Christ's final victory over the beast and the false church, the prostitute will suffer a major setback. For a long time the false church will enjoy the admiration of the world's masses. The prostitute sits; she occupies an impressive position over "peoples, multitudes, nations and languages" (verse 15). But then her illicit partner will turn on her: "The beast and the ten horns you saw will hate the prostitute" (verse 16). The beast will leave the prostitute "naked" (verse 16). She will be exposed for what she is, and then the beast will destroy her. This prophecy is fulfilled in our own age when atheistic governments oppose not only the true church, but also the false church. They don't want any mention of Christ within their borders, not even the false church's moralizing emphasis on good works.

All this happens by God's plan and allowance. He limits the power of the ten kings and puts "it into their hearts to accomplish his purpose" (verse 17). In the darkest days of the true church, the saints "know that in all things God works for the good of those who love him" (Romans 8:28). All the while the false church betrays Christ, struts its influence, and goes to bed with secular power, God is in control. In the end it is not the devil's wiles, the beast's power, or the woman's lies that prevail. "God's words are fulfilled" (verse 17).

The angel provides one final identification of the woman: "The woman you saw is the great city that rules over the kings of the earth" (verse 18). When we compare this verse to previous visions, we see that "the great city" is Babylon. Babylon stands for the combined antichristian forces in the world (14:8; 16:19; 17:5; 18:2,10). The woman who steers the beast is the driving power behind this force. The lie that we can please God by our good efforts divorces us from Christ and undermines his saving gospel.

Babylon's defeat

18 **After this I saw another angel coming down from heaven. He had great authority, and the earth was illuminated by his splendor. ²With a mighty voice he shouted:**

"Fallen! Fallen is Babylon the Great!
She has become a home for demons

and a haunt for every evil spirit,
a haunt for every unclean and detestable bird.
³ For all the nations have drunk
the maddening wine of her adulteries.
The kings of the earth committed adultery with her,
and the merchants of the earth grew rich
from her excessive luxuries."

⁴Then I heard another voice from heaven say:

"Come out of her, my people,
so that you will not share in her sins,
so that you will not receive any of her plagues;
⁵ for her sins are piled up to heaven,
and God has remembered her crimes.
⁶ Give back to her as she has given;
pay her back double for what she has done.
Mix her a double portion from her own cup.
⁷ Give her as much torture and grief
as the glory and luxury she gave herself.
In her heart she boasts,
'I sit as queen; I am not a widow,
and I will never mourn.'
⁸ Therefore in one day her plagues will overtake her:
death, mourning and famine.
She will be consumed by fire,
for mighty is the Lord God who judges her.

⁹"When the kings of the earth who committed adultery with her and shared her luxury see the smoke of her burning, they will weep and mourn over her. ¹⁰Terrified at her torment, they will stand far off and cry:

" 'Woe! Woe, O great city,
O Babylon, city of power!
In one hour your doom has come!'

¹¹"The merchants of the earth will weep and mourn over her because no one buys their cargoes any more—¹²cargoes of gold,

silver, precious stones and pearls; fine linen, purple, silk and scarlet cloth; every sort of citron wood, and articles of every kind made of ivory, costly wood, bronze, iron and marble; [13]cargoes of cinnamon and spice, of incense, myrrh, and frankincense, of wine and olive oil, of fine flour and wheat; cattle and sheep; horses and carriages; and bodies and souls of men. [14]"They will say, 'The fruit you longed for is gone from you. All your riches and splendor have vanished, never to be recovered.' [15]The merchants who sold these things and gained their wealth from her will stand far off, terrified at her torment. They will weep and mourn [16]and cry out:

> " 'Woe! Woe, O great city,
>   dressed in fine linen, purple and scarlet,
>   and glittering with gold, precious stones and pearls!
> [17] In one hour such great wealth has been brought to ruin!'

"Every sea captain, and all who travel by ship, the sailors, and all who earn their living from the sea, will stand far off. [18]When they see the smoke of her burning, they will exclaim, 'Was there ever a city like this great city?' [19]They will throw dust on their heads, and with weeping and mourning cry out:

> " 'Woe! Woe, O great city,
>   where all who had ships on the sea
>   became rich through her wealth!
>   In one hour she has been brought to ruin!
> [20] Rejoice over her, O heaven!
>   Rejoice, saints and apostles and prophets!
>   God has judged her for the way she treated you.' "

[21]Then a mighty angel picked up a boulder the size of a large millstone and threw it into the sea, and said:

> "With such violence
>   the great city of Babylon will be thrown down,
>   never to be found again.
> [22] The music of harpists and musicians,
>   flute players and trumpeters,
>   will never be heard in you again.

No workman of any trade
will ever be found in you again.
The sound of a millstone
will never be heard in you again.
²³ The light of a lamp
will never shine in you again.
The voice of bridegroom and bride
will never be heard in you again.
Your merchants were the world's great men.
By your magic spell all the nations were led astray.
²⁴ In her was found the blood of prophets and of the saints,
and of all who have been killed on the earth."

At the end of the last chapter, the angel said the prostitute on the beast was "the great city that rules over the kings of the earth" (17:18). The vision in chapter 18 is a poetic portrait of the demise of this great city, Babylon. The angel who announced the downfall of Babylon held a position of high authority in heaven. Only the greatest power in heaven can defeat the antichristian forces lined up against Christ's church. The angel's presence that "illuminated" (verse 1) the earth may symbolize an end to the darkness that the false church brought with its lies. His "mighty voice" (verse 2) signals the importance of his announcement.

Three of the seven visions in Revelation portray Babylon as the great enemy of Christ's church. Many of the images in this chapter echo the language of the previous two visions. The ancient city of Babylon lay in ruins when John wrote Revelation. But for a long time before it was destroyed, Babylon stood for everything that threatened God's people. It was rich, proud, powerful, and pagan. God used Babylon to chastise his Old Testament people for their unfaithfulness to him. First, God sent them into captivity in Babylon; then he brought back a remnant and established them in Jerusalem.

The first Babylon was gone, but John's readers, who knew the Old Testament, had a clear picture of what it represented. For God's people in the New Testament, Babylon represents every evil force that draws them away from Christ and seeks to enslave them.

John's readers in every age need to trust that God is greater than "Babylon the Great" (verse 2). The angel with the loud voice invites that trust with his announcement at the beginning of this chapter: "Fallen! Fallen is Babylon the Great" (verse 2). Following the angel with the eternal gospel in chapter 14, another angel made the identical announcement of the fall of Babylon (14:8). Those who believe in the gospel accept the defeat of the church's enemies as a foregone conclusion.

John is given a vision of a future time when antichristian forces will lie in ruins like the ancient city. The picture is of an uninhabited city with sand drifting through the remains of fallen buildings. This is the haunt of devils whom God has deprived of their victims. Jesus said, "When an evil spirit comes out of a man, it goes through arid places seeking rest and does not find it" (Matthew 12:43). God destroys Babylon for three reasons. She deceived most of the world with her "adulteries" (verse 3; see 14:8), her unfaithful teachings about Christ. She sinfully allied herself with worldly governments (see 17:3), and she forsook her spiritual treasure in pursuit of earthly riches (see 17:4).

"Another voice from heaven" (verse 4) issues a warning call to God's people. The driving force behind the enemies of the church is the lie that we can in some way earn or participate in our own salvation (see 17:18). Everywhere, Scripture urges us to separate ourselves from this false teaching. Isaiah urged God's people, "Touch no unclean thing! Come out from it and be pure" (Isaiah 52:11). Jesus said, "Watch out for false prophets" (Matthew 7:15). Paul wrote, "Watch out for those who cause divisions and put obstacles in your way that are contrary to the teaching you have learned. Keep away from them" (Romans 16:17). Separation from the false church always involves social, economic, or personal loss. But God's call to us to separate aims to prevent even greater harm, "so that you will not receive any of her plagues" (verse 4; see chapters 15,16).

The false church is smug. "She boasts, 'I sit as a queen; I am not a widow, and I will never mourn'" (verse 7). But God knows she has been destroying souls. "Her sins are piled up to heaven" (verse 5). In verses 6 and 7 we hear the voice of the angel calling out to God for perfect justice. For all the anguish she has caused, she will suffer anguish. The false church that refuses the free forgiveness offered in the gospel will suffer under the law's justice: "Show no pity: life for life, eye for eye, tooth for tooth, hand for hand, foot for foot" (Deuteronomy 19:21). Final justice will come in the fires of hell (see 14:10,11): "She will be consumed by fire" (verse 8).

In the final judgment those who allied themselves with Babylon will "weep and mourn over her" (verse 9). World leaders who governed by Satan's direction will be "terrified at her torment" (verse 10). Merchants who grew rich under the false church's philosophy of human accomplishment (verse 11) will also be "terrified at her torment" (verse 15). All the false church's allies will be amazed at how quickly— "in one hour" (verses 10,17,19)—her doom has come.

The sympathy the false church's allies display is shallow. What terrifies them is her sudden loss of worldly wealth and the prospect that they may now lose some of their own riches. The kings who "shared her luxury" (verse 9), the merchants who "gained their wealth from her" (verse 15), and the sea captains who "became rich through her wealth" (verse 19) exhibit no spiritual remorse. Their terror will intensify when they realize they are going to share her eternal punishment.

The voice that John heard from heaven (verse 4) invites the saints, victorious on the Last Day, to rejoice in God's punishment of Babylon (verses 20-24). This is not a song any of us will sing until the final judgment. Like Jesus, we will pray for our enemies and hope for their conversion. As long as this earth stands, we will share God's saving will with the church's worst enemies. "As surely as I live, declares the Sovereign LORD, I take no pleasure in the death of the wicked, but rather that they turn from their ways and live" (Ezekiel 33:11).

Even on the Last Day, no one will rejoice because the souls of those in the false church have been lost. Our joy will come from knowing that the elect no longer will have to suffer at the hand of their enemies. "God judged her for the way she treated you" (verse 20). Not one more soul will be drawn away from Jesus with the promise of earthly success and wealth. No more people will be offered the false confidence that, if they do their best, God will accept them.

God's judgment of Babylon is pictured as final and total. The angel with the boulder says, "The great city of Babylon will be thrown down, never to be found again" (verse 21). There is no sign of life left in the city: no musicians (verse 22), no workers (verse 22), no lamps in the windows (verse 23), no marriages (verse 23).

Babylon is the spirit of antichrist. It is most pronounced in the false church, but it infects all human institutions. Babylon's "magic spell" (verse 23) is the universally appealing teaching that salvation can be won by man's good works. "All the nations were led astray" (verse 23). To identify this "magic spell" around us, all we have to do is ask, "What do most people believe about how to get to heaven?"

When Babylon lies in ruins, we will find in her streets "the blood of prophets and of the saints" (verse 24). The false church cannot tolerate those who give simple witness to the blood and merit of Jesus. For this she will suffer forever.

The church's victory

The Lamb's wedding supper

19 After this I heard what sounded like the roar of a great multitude in heaven shouting:

"Hallelujah!
Salvation and glory and power belong to our God,
2   for true and just are his judgments.
He has condemned the great prostitute
    who corrupted the earth by her adulteries.
He has avenged on her the blood of his servants."

3And again they shouted:

"Hallelujah!
The smoke from her goes up for ever and ever."

4The twenty-four elders and the four living creatures fell down and worshiped God, who was seated on the throne. And they cried:

"Amen, Hallelujah!"

5Then a voice came from the throne, saying:

"Praise our God,
    all you his servants,
you who fear him,
    both small and great!"

6Then I heard what sounded like a great multitude, like the roar of rushing waters and like loud peals of thunder, shouting:

"Hallelujah!
For our Lord God Almighty reigns.
⁷ Let us rejoice and be glad
and give him glory!
For the wedding of the Lamb has come,
and his bride has made herself ready.
⁸ Fine linen, bright and clean, was given her to wear."
(Fine linen stands for the righteous acts of the saints.)

⁹Then the angel said to me, "Write: 'Blessed are those who are invited to the wedding supper of the Lamb!'" And he added, "These are the true words of God."
¹⁰At this I fell at his feet to worship him. But he said to me, "Do not do it! I am a fellow servant with you and with your brothers who hold to the testimony of Jesus. Worship God! For the testimony of Jesus is the spirit of prophecy."

At the Last Day, the angels called the saints to rejoice over Babylon's defeat (18:20-24). At the beginning of chapter 19, the scene changes from judgment day to heaven, but the celebration of victory over Babylon continues. John heard "what sounded like the roar of a great multitude in heaven" (verse 1). The 24 elders and the four living creatures (verse 4) are a part of this multitude. The 24 elders represent all the believers of the Old and New Testaments (see 4:4). The four living creatures symbolize all God's created world (see 4:6). The roaring sound reflects the multitude's great joy.

"Hallelujah" and its Greek spelling "alleluia" are a regular part of our Lutheran hymns and liturgy. Yet *hallelujah* occurs only four times in the New Testament—all four times in the first six verses of chapter 19. *Hallelujah* is a Hebrew word that means "Praise the Lord." *Hallelujah* expresses believers' appreciation of God's undeserved love to them. It is the opposite of self-glorification and work-righteousness. The ultimate joy of the saints is what God's grace and power did to defeat all their enemies.

The multitude shouts out, "Salvation and glory and power belong to our God" (verse 1). Most verses of praise in Revelation have three parts (4:8,11; 11:17; 12:10; 15:3,4; 16:5) in order to recognize the three persons of God. God deserves glory because he won salvation for his people by his power. The great multitude acknowledges that the judgment God dealt Babylon (see 18:5-8) is "true and just" (verse 2). Peter writes that false prophets "will be paid back with harm for the harm they have done" (2 Peter 2:13). Another hallelujah rises from the shouts of the multitude (verse 3) because their great enemy's defeat is final. Babylon will never again harm the saints (see 18:9,18).

During their shouts of hallelujah, the elders and the living creatures fell with their faces to the ground and worshiped God. They responded to the multitude's praise with "Amen, Hallelujah!" (verse 4). Their amen expresses hearty agreement to the shouts of praise: "Yes, it is true. God is to be praised for what he has done."

The elders represent all believers, and the living creatures represent the created world. It should not surprise us to see the created world join the saints in heaven to praise God. Paul told the Romans that the created world waits with believers to be delivered from the sin-ravaged earth. "The creation waits in eager expectation for the sons of God to be revealed. . . . The creation itself will be liberated from its bondage to decay and brought into the glorious freedom of the children of God" (Romans 8:19,21).

The angel's voice "from the throne" (verse 5; see verse 10) invites every voice in heaven to join the song of praise. The combined voices sound even louder than the "roar" (verse 1) John first heard. It is "like the roar of rushing waters and like loud peals of thunder" (verse 6). The fourth hallelujah begins their shout of praise. As the number 3 stands for God, the number 4 represents the earth and all God's creatures.

God has always been on his throne, ruling with love and power for his people. But now, for the first time, all God's creatures can see him reign. The once-persecuted saints are no longer tempted with doubts whether God is in control. It is time to "rejoice and be glad and give him glory!" (verse 7). Unlike Babylon's short-lived claims to authority (18:7), God's rule is eternal.

Heaven consummates the marriage of the Lamb to his bride, the church. Later, an angel provides John a beautiful vision of the new Jerusalem, "prepared as a bride beautifully dressed for her husband" (21:2). During our lives on earth, Jesus courts his bride and wins her over by his grace. Jesus gives his bride time to get ready for the great marriage feast of heaven.

Preparation for marriage to Christ is not something we can do by ourselves. The heavenly chorus shouts that "fine linen, bright and clean, was given her to wear" (verse 8). John quickly explains, "Fine linen stands for the righteous acts of the saints" (verse 8). But fine linen "was given" to the saints, so it cannot mean something they earned on their own. "The righteous acts" is the NIV translation for a single Greek word John used that is better translated "the righteous verdict." It does not refer to what the saints have done but to God's action of declaring sinners righteous for Jesus' sake. This correct understanding of the word better explains the linen that was given to the saints.

The marriage of the Lamb and his bride will be an eternally happy celebration. After the shouts of hallelujah, the angel told John to write, "Blessed are those who are invited to the wedding supper of the Lamb!" (verse 9). To be blessed is to be spiritually happy. In heaven sin and its consequences will never again disturb our souls. On this earth we get a taste of that happiness when Jesus comes close to us in his Word. Our Savior told us, "Blessed . . . are those who hear the word of God and obey it" (Luke 11:28).

Through every earthly disappointment, faith focuses on the future joys of heaven. The words of the angel stress the reality of heaven: "These are the true words of God" (verse 9). In the middle of their greatest fears, Jesus invited his disciples to think of heaven: "Do not let your hearts be troubled. Trust in God; trust also in me. In my Father's house are many rooms; if it were not so, I would have told you" (John 14:1,2). Every short-term goal we set our hopes on will disappoint us. So Jesus urged, "Store up for yourselves treasures in heaven, where moth and rust do not destroy, and where thieves do not break in and steal. For where your treasure is, there your heart will be also" (Matthew 6:21). Without doubt, this sure promise of heaven brought comfort to John's first readers, the persecuted believers in Asia Minor.

The voice of the angel who spoke to John (verse 9) first came from the throne (verse 5). John mistakenly thought that it was the voice of God. When John tried to worship him, the angel quickly stopped him: "Do not do it!" (verse 10). He explained that he was a servant of God like John. Although they live in the presence of God, angels are created beings. When they give "testimony of Jesus" (verse 10), they serve God the same way all Christians do. "Are not all angels ministering spirits sent to serve those who will inherit salvation?" (Hebrews 1:14).

John and the angel shared the same purpose. Both existed to tell people about Jesus. The closing words of the angel provide an important insight for us who share that work with them. "Worship God! For the testimony of Jesus is the spirit of prophecy," the angel said (verse 10). "Prophecy" is the task of every believer to explain and share the Scripture with others. The "spirit" of prophecy is the heart and soul of that Christian activity. The whole purpose for understanding the Bible and talking to others about it is to testify to Jesus.

Many well-meaning people—including many of the church's noted teachers—forget that the whole Bible points to Jesus. We are blessed to know that Jesus stands at the center of Scripture and to share that truth with others. The angel said that this is how we worship God. God is not worshiped when men or angels approach him by some avenue other than proclaiming Jesus from the Bible. Jesus said, "Whoever accepts me accepts the one who sent me" (John 13:20). When we help others to know the Jesus of the Bible, we also worship God.

The Rider on the white horse

¹¹I saw heaven standing open and there before me was a white horse, whose rider is called Faithful and True. With justice he judges and makes war. ¹²His eyes are like blazing fire, and on his head are many crowns. He has a name written on him that no one knows but he himself. ¹³He is dressed in a robe dipped in blood, and his name is the Word of God. ¹⁴The armies of heaven were following him, riding on white horses and dressed in fine linen, white and clean. ¹⁵Out of his mouth comes a sharp sword with which to strike down the nations. "He will rule them with an iron scepter." He treads the winepress of the fury of the wrath of God Almighty. ¹⁶On his robe and on his thigh he has this name written:

KING OF KINGS AND LORD OF LORDS.

¹⁷And I saw an angel standing in the sun, who cried in a loud voice to all the birds flying in midair, "Come, gather together for the great supper of God, ¹⁸so that you may eat the flesh of

kings, generals, and mighty men, of horses and their riders, and the flesh of all people, free and slave, small and great." [19]Then I saw the beast and the kings of the earth and their armies gathered together to make war against the rider on the horse and his army. [20]But the beast was captured, and with him the false prophet who had performed the miraculous signs on his behalf. With these signs he had deluded those who had received the mark of the beast and worshiped his image. The two of them were thrown alive into the fiery lake of burning sulfur. [21]The rest of them were killed with the sword that came out of the mouth of the rider on the horse, and all the birds gorged themselves on their flesh.

In the vision of the scroll we saw four horses and their riders (6:2-8). The first horse was white and, with its rider, symbolized the influence Jesus wields on earth through his Word. Now John sees another white horse with a rider. This time the rider is Jesus. The first horse and its rider rode through the earth in the middle of battle. This horse and rider are parading through heaven as victors.

Heaven stood open to reveal the rider whose name is Faithful and True (verse 11). God's faithfulness is like a double-edged sword: "Know therefore that the LORD your God is God; he is the faithful God, keeping his covenant of love to a thousand generations of those who love him and keep his commands. But those who hate him he will repay to their face by destruction" (Deuteronomy 7:9,10). Jesus is called True because he is consistent and loyal. To the Laodiceans Jesus introduced himself as "the Amen, the faithful and true witness" (3:14). Jesus does what he says. In the description that follows, we see that this rider will carry out both the promises and threats he makes in his Word.

"His eyes are like blazing fire, and on his head are many crowns" (verse 12). The blazing eyes and the crowns display

Jesus' omniscience and omnipotence. Jesus' blazing eyes will see through every hypocrisy. Paul described the final judgment as "the day when God will judge men's secrets through Jesus Christ" (Romans 2:16). The crowns on his head are diadems, a symbol of divinity and absolute power (see 13:1). What his enemies once presumed to wear, Jesus deserves to wear.

The decisions our Lord makes on judgment day will be perfect. "With justice he judges and makes war" (verse 11). The Faithful and True will not change the rules at the end. On earth he said, "There is a judge for the one who rejects me and does not accept my words; that very word which I spoke will condemn him at the last day" (John 12:48). At the Last Day Jesus will judge and wage eternal war against his enemies "with justice" (verse 11). As terrible as the fate of his enemies will be, it will be perfectly fair. Many think that a loving God could not design a horrible place like hell. They do not take into account the damning nature of sin and God's anger. A holy God demands justice that displays both his love of good and his hatred of evil.

The rider of the white horse "has a name written on him that no one knows but he himself" (verse 12). Earlier, Jesus promised the saints at Pergamum that he would give them "a white stone with a new name written on it, known only to him who receives it" (2:17). *Name* in Scripture often has the broader meaning of reputation, that is, what is known about a person. Only in heaven will the believer fully appreciate all that Jesus is. "Now we see but a poor reflection as in a mirror; then we shall see face to face. Now I know in part; then I shall know fully, even as I am fully known" (1 Corinthians 13:12). While we wait for heaven, we will not press for an explanation of the name of Jesus beyond what he has told us in his Word.

The name of the rider of the white horse is "the Word of God" (verse 13). From eternity to eternity, all we know about Jesus is identical with what we know about the Word of God. "In the beginning . . . the Word was with God" (John 1:1). "By the word of the LORD were the heavens made" (Psalm 33:6), yet "all things" (John 1:3; Colossians 1:16) were made by Jesus. By his Word God promised the Savior through the Old Testament prophets, and that "Word became flesh and made his dwelling among us" (John 1:14). "By the same word the present heaven and earth are reserved for fire, being kept for the day of judgment and destruction of ungodly men" (2 Peter 3:7). Jesus is the Word of God that his enemies will see riding the white horse of victory.

The great prostitute "was drunk with the blood of the saints" (17:6). In Babylon "was found the blood of prophets and the saints" (18:24). Now the rider on the white horse has taken vengeance on all the blood shed by the enemies of the church. "He is dressed in a robe dipped in blood" (verse 13). This pictures the hem of a victor's cloak that becomes stained with blood as he walks among his enemies slain on the battlefield.

"The armies of heaven" (verse 14) that follow the rider on the white horse are the angels that fought for the saints (see 12:7-11). "When the Son of Man comes in his glory, and all the angels with him, he will sit on his throne in heavenly glory" (Matthew 25:31). The white linen the angels wore signifies the purity of the holy angels (Mark 8:38).

Jesus said that he would return "with great power and glory" (Mark 13:26). The army of angels demonstrates the glory of his final victory. His power is pictured as a "sharp sword with which to strike down the nations" (verse 15). This is the same powerful Word of God that Jesus uses on earth (see 1:16). In eternity the rule of his Word will be absolute: "He will rule them with an iron scepter" (verse 15). In eternity Jesus will carry out the full judgment of this prophecy made by the psalmist (Psalm 2:9).

In an earlier vision of the last judgment, the enemies of the church "were trampled in the winepress of God's wrath" (14:20). In that vision we were not told who did the trampling. Now John sees that the avenger is Jesus: "He treads the winepress of the fury of the wrath of God Almighty." This is a stern reminder. The patience God shows to sinners must never be mistaken for leniency. The punishment he holds back to allow us time to repent will one day be carried out in full on the unrepentant.

In plain sight, where all his enemies could read it, Jesus wore the name "KING OF KINGS AND LORD OF LORDS" (verse 16). This does not refer to Jesus' rule over the worldly kings mentioned in verse 18. This name means Jesus is the King and Lord of the saints. Believers are the kings for whom Jesus is the King. We are the lords who will serve the Lord forever. We share in his final judgment and eternal rule. For he promised us, "I confer on you a kingdom, just as my Father conferred one on me, so that you may eat and drink at my table in my kingdom and sit on thrones, judging the twelve tribes of Israel" (Luke 22:29,30; see Revelation 1:6). Alongside Jesus "the saints will judge the world" (1 Corinthians 6:2). "If we endure, we will also reign with him" (2 Timothy 2:12).

In the next scene, an angel was "standing in the sun" (verse 17) so that all the birds in the sky could hear his invitation to devour what is left of the dead bodies of the church's enemies. The scene is a battlefield strewn with decaying bodies of soldiers after a massive defeat. Jesus will cause quick and thorough destruction of his enemies when he returns. Our Lord himself prophesied this scene: "For as lightning that comes from the east is visible even in the west, so will be the coming of the Son of Man. Wherever there is a carcass, there the vultures will gather" (Matthew 24:27,28). The fact that the angel calls to the birds before the battle begins in the next verse indicates that Jesus' victory is a foregone conclusion.

The defeat of the great enemies of the church already has been announced, but they gather "to make war against the rider on the horse and his army" (verse 19). Although John describes the appearance of the rider and the battle in some detail (verses 11-21), all these events take place in a few moments on judgment day. As quickly as Jesus' enemies align themselves against him, they are defeated.

First, the beast was captured (verse 20). This is the beast from the sea that symbolizes all earthly governments Satan manipulates for his purposes (see 13:1-10). Then the false prophet "who had performed the miraculous signs on his behalf" also was captured (verse 20). This false prophet is the second beast, the beast from the earth that represents the false church and its unholy alliances with secular power (see 13:11-18). These beasts, both allies of the "enormous red dragon" (12:3), Satan, will be "thrown alive into the fiery lake of burning sulfur" (verse 20). John has used burning sulfur before to picture the torment of hell (see 14:10).

All those that followed the two beasts "were killed with the sword that came out of the mouth of the rider on the horse" (verse 21). This sword is the Word of God, the same one we saw when the rider on the horse first appeared (verse 15). We note that this is not the double-edged sword of law and gospel that Jesus wielded on earth (see 1:16). Those who put their hope in the false church's teaching of work-righteousness and refuse Jesus will not hear the gospel message again. It is too late for that. This is the Last Day. They will hear only the law's judgment on their sins and unbelief.

VISION OF FINAL VICTORY
(20:1–22:5)

Satan's final defeat

20 And I saw an angel coming down out of heaven, having the key to the Abyss and holding in his hand a great chain. ²He seized the dragon, that ancient serpent, who is the devil, or Satan, and bound him for a thousand years. ³He threw him into the Abyss, and locked and sealed it over him, to keep him from deceiving the nations anymore until the thousand years were ended. After that, he must be set free for a short time.

⁴I saw thrones on which were seated those who had been given authority to judge. And I saw the souls of those who had been beheaded because of their testimony for Jesus and because of the word of God. They had not worshiped the beast or his image and had not received his mark on their foreheads or their hands. They came to life and reigned with Christ a thousand years. ⁵(The rest of the dead did not come to life until the thousand years were ended.) This is the first resurrection. ⁶Blessed and holy are those who have part in the first resurrection. The second death has no power over them, but they will be priests of God and of Christ and will reign with him for a thousand years.

⁷When the thousand years are over, Satan will be released from his prison ⁸and will go out to deceive the nations in the four corners of the earth—Gog and Magog—to gather them for battle. In number they are like the sand on the seashore. ⁹They marched across the breadth of the earth and surrounded the camp of God's people, the city he loves. But fire came down from heaven and devoured them. ¹⁰And the devil, who deceived them, was thrown into the lake of burning sulfur, where the

beast and the false prophet had been thrown. They will be tormented day and night for ever and ever.

An angel introduces John to the seventh and last vision in Revelation. We can tell that this is a new vision because John is taken backward in time. The last vision ended on the day of judgment with Jesus' final victory over his enemies. The seventh vision takes us back to the beginning of the New Testament age.

The angel came "down out of heaven" (verse 1). He came down because "the great dragon was hurled down—that ancient serpent called the devil, or Satan, who leads the whole world astray" (12:9). The angel has "the key to the Abyss" (verse 1). This identifies him as Jesus. Jesus already told John that he holds "the keys of death and Hades" (1:18). The great chain that Jesus carries in his hand (verse 1) symbolizes his power to leash and curb the devil.

Jesus bound the devil for a thousand years. This "thousand years" (verse 2) has been mishandled more than any word of Scripture. Millenialists (*millennium* means a thousand) hold that it refers to a thousand years at the end of the world when believers will rule on this earth and defeat all their enemies. Many other false ideas and predictions have arisen from taking this thousand years in a literal way.

How can we be sure that this "thousand years" must not be understood literally? First, every phrase in verses 1 and 2 is figurative. John is in the middle of a vision. He pictures Jesus as an angel. He introduces the devil as a dragon. He speaks of hell as a deep pit, the Abyss. Although an abyss does not have a lock, John envisions Jesus holding a key. Satan is an evil spirit who cannot be held with chains, yet John pictures Jesus holding back Satan with a great chain. To take the thousand years at the end of verse 2 literally violates the way Jesus is speaking here through John.

There is a second reason why we cannot understand this thousand years literally. If there is any doubt about the meaning of a passage of Scripture, a believer allows the Bible to interpret itself. If there is any doubt about the meaning of the thousand years in this figurative passage, we must go to back to Jesus' literal descriptions of the last days in the Gospels. Our Lord's clear words there speak against a literal thousand years of Christian domination and universal peace.

In the Gospels Jesus speaks against the notion that there will be peace on earth and political rule by believers. He predicted the opposite in very literal terms. Jesus said the last days would be characterized by "wars and rumors of wars. . . . Nation will rise against nation, and kingdom against kingdom" (Matthew 24:6,7). Christians would not rule the earth, Jesus said, but would be turned over to rulers "to be persecuted and put to death" (Matthew 24:9). Instead of the mass conversions that millenialists predict, Jesus said there will be "many false prophets" and "the love of most will grow cold" (Matthew 24:11,12).

The rest of Scripture also rules out a literal thousand years of "heaven on earth." Paul wrote, "Now, brothers, about times and dates we do not need to write to you, for you know very well that the day of the Lord will come like a thief in the night. While people are saying, 'Peace and safety,' destruction will come on them suddenly" (1 Thessalonians 5:1-3). Peter also pointed his readers away from an earthly paradise. "In keeping with his promise," he wrote, "we are looking forward to a new heaven and a new earth, the home of righteousness" (2 Peter 3:13).

What is the thousand years of verse 2? Since it begins with the binding of Satan (verse 2) and ends with the devil's release for a short time (verse 3), the thousand years is the New Testament age. The New Testament age began with the coming of Christ. "The reason the Son of God appeared was to destroy the devil's work" (1 John 3:8). During his earthly ministry Jesus announced, "The prince of this world now stands condemned" (John 16:11). By his death and resurrection Jesus "disarmed the power and authorities" (Colossians 2:15). The binding of Satan—the limiting of his ability to hurt God's people—marked the beginning of the thousand years, the beginning of the New Testament age.

Millennium was the name of the largest number in a Greek's vocabulary. "A thousand" seemed like an interminable number. In verse 3 "a thousand" symbolizes the unspecified length of the New Testament age during which Satan would be bound. At the beginning of the world, Jude wrote, God limited the activity of the evil angels when he expelled them from heaven. They were "bound with everlasting chains for judgment on the great Day" (Jude 6). The story of Job illustrates how God—already in the Old Testament—restrained Satan's power.

The sealing of the Abyss in verse 3 indicates the greater restriction on demonic activity that Jesus' victory ushered in for the New Testament age. Neither the binding of Satan at the beginning of the world or his binding during the New Testament age completely restricts the devil. This is clear from Scripture's many warnings about Satan's prowess. The chain and the pit serve as a leash that holds in check Satan's attacks against the church.

Near the end of the New Testament age, the devil will be "set free for a short time" (verse 3). This relatively short time will mark a period of great distress for believers. During those last days "false prophets will appear and deceive many people" and "the love of most will grow cold" (Matthew 24:11,12). Jesus said, "If those days had not been cut short, no one would survive, but for the sake of the elect those days will be shortened" (Matthew 24:22).

In verses 4 to 6 John's attention is drawn to thrones of judgment in heaven. Seated on these thrones were the saints and martyrs. These are the faithful who "had not worshiped the beast or his image and had not received his mark on their foreheads or their hands" (verse 4). In an earlier vision John identified those who worshiped the beast as unbelievers— "all whose names have not been written in the book of life belonging to the Lamb" (13:8). In the same way, those with the mark of the beast are those who collaborated with worldly powers against the Lamb (13:11-18).

In verse 4 John records no passing of time between Satan's binding and the activity around the thrones. So those sitting on thrones of judgment represent those who died in faith during the New Testament age. John's first readers, no doubt, saw or heard about fellow Christians who were persecuted and put to death for their faith. They were "beheaded because of their testimony for Jesus and because of the word of God" (verse 4). We, along with Revelation's first readers in Asia Minor, may have the comfort that those who die in faith are alive in heaven now. Even before the final judgment, they rule with Christ.

This truth is reinforced for us when John writes that he saw the "souls" of those who had been beheaded (verse 4). He saw only the souls of departed believers on thrones of judgment because their bodies would not be raised to life and reunited with their souls until the resurrection.

At the end of verse 4, we read that "they came to life and reigned with Christ a thousand years." John's actual words are not "they *came to life*" but simply "they *lived* and reigned with Christ." This more careful translation contradicts the view of some millenialists that there will be two physical resurrections of believers, one at the beginning of a millennium and another at the final judgment. The words John uses echo an important Bible truth. The souls of believers do not have to be resurrected because they never really die; they never cease to exist. Jesus promised Martha, "Whoever lives and believes in me will never die" (John 11:26), and he assured the thief on the cross, "I tell you the truth, today you will be with me in paradise" (Luke 23:43). Those who die with Christ begin to reign immediately with him through the thousand years of the New Testament age.

That reign includes judging the evil angels and the unbelievers. Paul told the Corinthians that the saints would judge the world and angels (1 Corinthians 6:2,3). The judging in verse 4 refers neither to judgment day nor to the reign of believers in eternity after judgment day. This judging begins the moment our souls are taken to heaven. Believers continue to live and reign with Christ when their souls leave their bodies.

That is not true of unbelievers. John calls unbelievers "the rest of the dead" (verse 5). The NIV translation again is not accurate. John did not write, "The rest of the dead did not *come to life*" (verse 5). He wrote that they "*did not live*" until the thousand years were ended. Those who die without Christ are dead, body and soul, until the resurrection. When Christ raises their bodies and reunites them with their souls, they will live again for a short time, only to face the final judgment and eternal death.

For us as believers, living and reigning with Christ begins when we come to faith. In baptism, Paul says, we were buried with Christ in order that, through faith, we will also live with him (Romans 6:4-8). Conversion is resurrection from spiritual death. When we came to faith, "God raised us up with Christ and seated us with him in the heavenly realms" (Ephesians 2:6).

Jesus also spoke about coming to faith as coming to life. He said, "I tell you the truth, a time is coming and has now come when the dead will hear the voice of the Son of God and those who hear will live" (John 5:25). At the end of verse 5, John speaks of "the first resurrection." Since John saw only the souls of believers in heaven, this first resurrection cannot mean the bodily resurrection of believers before the Last Day. It means the believer's resurrection from spiritual death through conversion.

Those who are resurrected to faith in Jesus are "blessed and holy" (verse 6). "Blessed" means happy. In the Bible blessedness does not mean worldly happiness but the inner peace that comes from knowing Jesus. Since we learn of Jesus in the Bible, Jesus said, "Blessed . . . are those who hear the word of God and obey it" (Luke 11:28). Believers are spiritually happy because through faith in Jesus they are holy. Their sins are forgiven, and Jesus clothes them with his righteousness (see 3:4,5).

Those who are happy and holy in Jesus will not be affected by "the second death" (verse 6). The first death was the spiritual death into which we were born. "You were dead in your transgressions and sins" (Ephesians 2:1). The first resurrection is conversion. The second death is what unbelievers face when they die. Physical death without faith ends in eternal death. The second death has no power over believers. They go from living and reigning with Christ in this world to living and reigning with Christ on thrones of judgment in heaven.

The thousand years that verse 6 refers to is not eternity. It is the same reign and rule of the souls of believers with Christ until the end of the New Testament age that is described in verses 4 and 5. For those who die in faith, the priestly work and reign that begin at conversion (see 1:5,6) continue uninterrupted until the Last Day. The second death has no power to change our relationship to Christ.

The thousand-year period that began at verse 1 ends at verse 7. In verse 3 John told us how the New Testament age would end. The dragon would "be set free for a short time." Now we get the details. "Satan will be released from his prison and will go out to deceive the nations" (verses 7,8). These are the last terrible days for the earth. Paul described the results of Satan's release:

> There will be terrible times in the last days. People will be lovers of themselves, lovers of money, boastful, proud, abusive, disobedient to their parents, ungrateful, unholy, without love, unforgiving, slanderous, without self-control, brutal, not lovers of the good, treacherous, rash, conceited, lovers of pleasure rather than lovers of God (2 Timothy 3:1-5).

Deception is Satan's tool. "When he lies," Jesus said, "he speaks his native language, for he is a liar and the father of lies" (John 8:44). He deceived Eve and Adam at the beginning, and he will lie to the nations at the end. The four corners of the earth emphasize the universal influence of the devil. John borrows Ezekiel's references to "Gog and Magog" (verse 8; see Ezekiel 38,39) to describe all the rulers and nations that oppose God's people.

This description of the last times fits the days in which we are now living. Satan has deceived the nations and gathered them for battle against believers. His forces seem insurmountable: "In number they are like the sand on the seashore" (verse 8). They surround "the camp of God's people" (verse 9). But for those who live during these days, John provides ample comfort. First, he says that Satan's influence at the end of the New Testament age will be only "for a short time" (verse 3). He describes God's surrounded people as "the city he loves" (verse 9). And just when Satan's forces seem poised for their final victory, God intervenes with his final deliverance.

God's people are saved when God sends fire from heaven and destroys Satan and his allies (verse 9). Fire is the agent of God's anger against his enemies. Those who worship the beast will suffer by fire (14:10,11). The prostitute on the beast will be burned (17:16). Smoke will rise from Babylon forever (19:3). The beast and the false prophet will be "thrown alive into the fiery lake of burning sulfur" (19:20). Now, in his final act of avenging justice, God will destroy the devil who made them all do his bidding. "The devil, who deceived them, was thrown into the lake of burning sulfur" (verse 10).

Even this horrible scene provides comfort for the believer. John views the final destruction of Satan and the church's enemies as an accomplished fact. He records it in the past tense as though it had already taken place. In these last days we find confidence in John's inspired words. We need not doubt that we are "the camp of God's people, the city he loves" (verse 9).

We also take comfort from the contrast between the events at the close of this chapter and the description of eternal bliss in chapter 21. Satan, the beast, and the false prophet "will be tormented day and night for ever and ever" (verse 10). While we live in the sure hope of an end to our suffering, our enemies live in constant fear of suffering without end. Even in the darkest days for the church, every believer lives with the confidence of victory.

Jesus' final judgment

[11]Then I saw a great white throne and him who was seated on it. Earth and sky fled from his presence, and there was no place for them. [12]And I saw the dead, great and small, standing before the throne, and books were opened. Another book was opened, which is the book of life. The dead were judged according to what they had done as recorded in the books. [13]The sea gave up the dead that were in it, and death and Hades gave up the dead that were in them, and each person was judged according to what he had done. [14]Then death and Hades were thrown into the lake of fire. The lake of fire is the second death. [15]If anyone's name was not found written in the book of life, he was thrown into the lake of fire.

Immediately after the destruction of Satan and his forces comes the final judgment. The phrase "a great white throne" (verse 11) tells us that God is seated on the throne. John first saw the throne of God in chapters 4 and 5. At the final judgment the throne appears great and white. "White" signifies the holiness of the one sitting on the throne and the perfect justice he is about to dispense. Earth and sky represent all the powers of the natural world. Their swift departure from God's presence demonstrates God's overwhelming power and his ability to carry out his judgments. No power in heaven or on earth can save his enemies from his wrath.

The judgment begins. All the dead, "great and small" (verse 12), must appear before God. "We will all stand before God's judgment seat" (Romans 14:10). Neither our status nor our job on earth will gain preferential treatment for us before a holy and just God. God's perfect fairness at the last judgment leads believers to treat their neighbor fairly in this life. "You know that he who is both their Master and yours is in heaven, and there is no favoritism with him" (Ephesians 6:9).

God will read from two sets of books. First John says, "books were opened" (verse 12). Then he quickly adds, "Another book was opened, which is the book of life" (verse 12). The first set of books is the record of the lives of unbelievers. The fact that there is more than one book for them may reflect the fact that there are many more unbelievers than believers. "Wide is the gate and broad is the road that leads to destruction, and many enter through it. But small is the gate and narrow the road that leads to life, and only a few find it" (Matthew 7:13).

There is only one book for the believers, "which is the book of life" (20:12). Jesus promised each faithful member at Sardis that he would "never blot out his name from the book of life" (3:5). Those whose names are written in the book of life belong "to the Lamb that was slain from the creation of the world" (13:8). They are the elect, those whom God chose "from the creation of the world" (17:8).

"The dead were judged according to what they had done as recorded in the books" (verse 12). "The dead" here means the unbelieving. They are the "rest of the dead" (verse 5) who came to life at the end of the thousand years. But they are alive only in the sense that their bodies have been raised and joined with their souls. John refers to them as "the dead" even after the resurrection because their judgment of eternal death is sealed. Once physical death removes the opportunity for conversion, the second death is an uninterrupted condition. John views physical death, Hades, and the lake of fire as one continuing state of death.

All the dead are gathered from the sea, from death, and from Hades (verse 13). No matter how or where people die, they will have to face the judgment. "Hades" means hell, the place of suffering for the damned. Here "Hades" is the place where unbelievers' souls suffer until their bodies are raised at the Last Day. This becomes clear when John says that death and Hades are thrown into the lake of fire (verse 14). The lake of fire is the eternal hell following the judgment. All temporary states of death will be folded into eternal torment.

"The lake of fire is the second death" (verse 14). Here John says the second death, first mentioned in this chapter in verse 6, is an eternity in hell. All death is separation. Spiritual death, or unbelief, separates the soul from God even while the body is alive on earth. Physical death separates the soul from the body. Eternal death is the permanent separation of the body and soul from God. John never mentions the first death, but since the first resurrection is conversion (see verse 5), the first death must be spiritual death, or unbelief.

Twice John writes that the dead will be "judged according to what [they have] done" (verses 12,13). Those who refuse what Jesus has done for them will be judged on the basis of their own actions. No matter how good they were, they will fall short of God's demand for perfection. "No one will be declared righteous in his sight by observing the law" (Romans 3:20). Only those who by faith claim a righteousness better than their own will stand before the judge. Only those washed by the blood of the Lamb and clothed in his righteousness have their names in the book of life. "If anyone's name was not found written in the book of life, he was thrown into the lake of fire" (verse 15).

Description of heaven

The new heaven and new earth

21 Then I saw a new heaven and a new earth, for the first heaven and the first earth had passed away, and there was no longer any sea. [2]I saw the Holy City, the New Jerusalem, coming down out of heaven from God, prepared as a bride beautifully dressed for her husband. ³And I heard a loud voice from the throne saying, "Now the dwelling of God is with men, and he will live with them. They will be his people, and God himself will be with them and be their God. ⁴He will wipe every tear from their eyes. There will be no more death or mourning or crying or pain, for the old order of things has passed away."

⁵He who was seated on the throne said, "I am making everything new!" Then he said, "Write this down, for these words are trustworthy and true."

⁶He said to me: "It is done. I am the Alpha and the Omega, the Beginning and the End. To him who is thirsty I will give to drink without cost from the spring of the water of life. ⁷He who overcomes will inherit all this, and I will be his God and he will be my son. ⁸But the cowardly, the unbelieving, the vile, the murderers, the sexually immoral, those who practice magic arts, the idolaters and all liars—their place will be in the fiery lake of burning sulfur. This is the second death."

This shift of scenes is more abrupt than any other in Revelation. As horrifying as the eternal lake of fire was, so John's vision of heaven is exalting. It has inspired hymnwriters, comforted mourners at Christian burials, and held out hope to suffering Christians for nearly two thousand years. This beautiful description of life in the presence of God crowns the seventh vision and provides the glorious finale to all the visions Jesus gave John.

John saw "a new heaven and a new earth" (verse 1). Throughout this closing scene, literal and figurative descriptions of paradise stand side by side. It is not always easy to tell whether John is providing us a painting or a snapshot of heaven. This is also true of the opening statement about a new earth and sky. Will our earth and sky be destroyed and entirely new ones be created? Will our present world, as we know it, be destroyed and a renewed earth be our eternal home? It is also possible that John's words are highly figurative. A new heaven and earth may be his picture for an entirely new place that we call heaven.

The rest of Scripture leaves these questions unanswered. Peter writes, "The heavens will disappear with a roar; the elements will be destroyed by fire, and the earth and everything in it will be laid bare. But in keeping with his promise we are looking forward to a new heaven and a new earth, the home of righteousness" (2 Peter 3:10,13). Jesus said, "Heaven and earth will pass away" (Luke 21:33). Peter's words also speak of the destruction of the earth. Yet when he says, "It will be laid bare" (2 Peter 3:10), he allows the impression that it will not be total destruction or annihilation.

When the writer to the Hebrews addresses this question, he also provides some perspective for those who seek an answer: "Now he has promised, 'Once more I will shake not only the earth but also the heavens.' The words 'once more' indicate the removing of what can be shaken—that is, created things—so that what cannot be shaken may remain. Therefore, since we are receiving a kingdom that cannot be shaken, let us be thankful, and so worship God acceptably with reverence and awe" (Hebrews 12:26-28).

The new heaven and earth are not meant to answer our curiosity about the afterlife. But they do make two important points. God will destroy the earth we know now, so we should not set our hope on it. Gone with the old world was the sea (verse 1). The sea was where the first beast came from (chapter 13). Along with the destruction of the old world came the end of antichristian threats. God will provide a new place that is safe and unshakable. Rather than demanding that our curiosity be satisfied, our response should be reverent worship (see 2 Peter 3:11,12,14).

John saw "the Holy City, the new Jerusalem, coming down out of heaven from God" (verse 2). Just as the city of Babylon represents all the forces of Satan and unbelief, so the city of God in Revelation stands for all believers. Jesus said that on everyone who overcomes he would write "the name of the city of my God, the new Jerusalem, which is coming down out of heaven from my God" (3:12). This "Holy City" is the holy Christian church, "the camp of God's people, the city he loves" (20:9).

Already in the Old Testament, holy writers spoke of Jerusalem figuratively as the place where God was present among his people. Paul distinguished between the earthly city of Jerusalem and the heavenly one: "the Jerusalem that is above is free, and she is our mother" (Galatians 4:26). The writer to the Hebrews said that believers belong to God's "Holy City" already in this life: "You have come to Mount Zion, to the heavenly Jerusalem, the city of the living God" (12:22).

Paul taught that the church was Christ's bride (Ephesians 5:25-33). Heaven is the consummation of that marriage. There the church will be presented to her Lord "as a bride beautifully dressed for her husband" (verse 2). The dress she wears, of course, is the one her bridegroom presented to her. Jesus promised that believers "will walk with me, dressed in white, for they are worthy" (3:4). "Christ loved the church and gave himself up for her to make her holy, cleansing her by the washing with water through the word, and to present her to himself as a radiant church, without stain or wrinkle or any other blemish, but holy and blameless" (Ephesians 5:25-27).

John heard a loud voice from the throne (verse 3). The throne was God's throne, but the voice was the voice of an angel, as it was in chapter 19, verses 5 and 10. Little figurative language is in the angel's announcement. To the assembled saints he announces the beginning of endless bliss. His words provide a concise, yet most comforting, description of heaven. The many images of heaven that follow beautify the angel's description of paradise, yet add nothing to it.

When we arrive in heaven we will hear these words: "Now the dwelling of God is with men" (verse 3). God literally pitches his tent among us. This picture of a tent is borrowed from the Old Testament tabernacle, where God promised his presence among his people. John used the same imagery at the beginning of his gospel when he wrote of Jesus' coming into this world: "The Word became flesh and made his dwelling among us" (John 1:14).

God's tent in verse 3, however, denotes nothing temporary about his stay with us. Rather, it signifies that God will live right next to us as he never has before. "He will live with them. They will be his people, and God himself will be with them and be their God" (verse 3). God is always everywhere, but in heaven we will experience his perfect blessed presence. Jesus prayed that all believers "may be one, Father, just as you are in me and I am in you. May they also be in us" (John 17:21). On earth our sins and sorrows make this unity with God less than crystal clear to us. "Now we see but a poor reflection as in a mirror; then we shall see face to face" (1 Corinthians 13:12). In heaven, however, the unclarity will be gone. Face to face with God, with his tent pitched next to ours, we will enjoy his company in perfection.

In heaven all the earthly things that cloud our vision of God will be gone. Gone will be all sorrows. "God will wipe every tear from their eyes" (verse 4). "You will weep and mourn while the world rejoices," Jesus said. "You will grieve, but your grief will turn to joy" (John 16:20). There will be no tears in heaven because God will eliminate all the things that cause us sorrow on earth. "The old order of things has passed away" (verse 4) literally means all the things that existed before are gone. "There will be no more death or mourning or crying or pain" (verse 4). The saints stand before God washed in the blood of the Lamb and white with his holiness. Since there is no sin in heaven, all the grief that sin produced on earth will be absent.

Now Jesus speaks. John identifies him simply as "he who was seated on the throne" (verse 5). The voice was Jesus' voice. In the previous scene of this vision (20:11-15), the throne was the place from which the dead were judged. The Bible always identifies Jesus as the judge on the Last Day. Furthermore, the voice from the throne identifies himself with the same words Jesus used at the beginning of Revelation: "I am the Alpha and the Omega" (1:8).

Jesus confirmed the words of the angel. He tells the saints that they have passed from grace to glory. During their time of grace on earth, Satan was always prowling and sin took its toll. Now Jesus says, "I am making everything new!" (verse 5). Everything that threatened their happiness and made earth a temporary home is gone. Everything the saints experience in glory will be new.

As he has done many times before, Jesus asked John to record his words. Then he turned to John and said, "It is done. I am the Alpha and the Omega, the Beginning and the End" (verse 6). This phrase ascribes changelessness and faithfulness to Jesus. It makes him one with the God who identified himself to Moses as "I am who I am" (Exodus 3:14). "Jesus Christ is the same yesterday and today and forever" (Hebrews 13:7). Because Jesus does not change, he keeps his promises. He will do what he says. Because Jesus promised, "In my Father's house are many rooms" (John 14:2), there will be a real heaven. If Jesus says it will be, "It is done" (verse 6). Jesus gave John this description of himself not only to comfort the troubled Christians in Asia Minor but also for the benefit of all who wait for him to fulfill his promises.

In heaven we will drink from "the spring of the water of life" (verse 6). This promise of Jesus is nearly identical to the promise he made to the woman at Jacob's well: "Whoever drinks the water I give him will never thirst. Indeed, the water I give him will become in him a spring of water welling up to eternal life" (John 4:14). Jesus adds that the saints would "drink without cost" (verse 6). This addition recalls Isaiah's promise of salvation: "Come, all you who are thirsty, come to the waters; and you who have no money, come, buy and eat! Come, buy wine and milk without money and without cost" (Isaiah 55:1).

Jesus himself is the Water of life that sustains us in this world and the next (see 7:16,17). He won our salvation and offers it to us by grace, without cost. Throughout eternity our lives will be sustained by this living water. What Jesus did for us will have brought us to heaven and his grace will keep us there. All tortured souls who think they must do something more to get to heaven find peace in this Word of Christ. Salvation is "the gift of God—not by works" (Ephesians 2:8,9).

At the end of each letter to the seven churches in chapters 2 and 3, Jesus made a promise to him "who overcomes." Heaven is the fulfillment of those promises. Already on earth we know that we are "all sons of God through faith in Christ Jesus" (Galatians 3:26). Yet on earth sin diminishes our appreciation of that relationship to God. Those who overcome will enjoy "all this" (verse 7), all the joys of heaven. Yet the highest joy will be to hear our Savior say, "I will be his God, and he will be my son" (verse 7).

Excluded from the joy of God's sons and daughters are those who refused the living water in this life. Most of the list mentions people who were involved in coarse, outward sins. "Neither the sexually immoral nor idolaters nor adulterers nor male prostitutes nor homosexual offenders nor thieves nor the greedy nor drunkards nor slanderers nor swindlers will inherit the kingdom of God" (1 Corinthians 6:9,10). Open sins against God's law are evidence that there is no repentance. But leading the list are those who sin against the gospel, "the cowardly, the unbelieving" (verse 8). The cowardly give up their faith because they fear persecution. The unbelieving die without the water of life.

"Nice" people who die without Christ go to hell along with coarse sinners. "Their place" is the "fiery lake of burning sulfur" (verse 8). They share that place with their earthly allies. "The devil, who deceived them, was thrown into the lake of burning sulfur, where the beast and the false prophet had been thrown" (20:10). The first death, unbelief, can be overcome by drinking the water of life, the gospel of Jesus. But the second death is eternal (see 20:14).

The new Jerusalem

⁹One of the seven angels who had the seven bowls full of the seven last plagues came and said to me, "Come, I will show you the bride, the wife of the Lamb." ¹⁰And he carried me away in the Spirit to a mountain great and high, and showed me the Holy City, Jerusalem, coming down out of heaven from God. ¹¹It shone with the glory of God, and its brilliance was like that of a very precious jewel, like a jasper, clear as crystal. ¹²It had a great, high wall with twelve gates, and with twelve angels at the gates. On the gates were written the names of the twelve tribes of Israel. ¹³There were three gates on the east, three on the north, three on the south and three on the west. ¹⁴The wall of the city had twelve foundations, and on them were the names of the twelve apostles of the Lamb.

¹⁵The angel who talked with me had a measuring rod of gold to measure the city, its gates and its walls. ¹⁶The city was laid

out like a square, as long as it was wide. He measured the city with the rod and found it to be 12,000 stadia in length, and as wide and high as it is long. [17]He measured its wall and it was 144 cubits thick, by man's measurement, which the angel was using. [18]The wall was made of jasper, and the city of pure gold, as pure as glass. [19]The foundations of the city walls were decorated with every kind of precious stone. The first foundation was jasper, the second sapphire, the third chalcedony, the fourth emerald, [20]the fifth sardonyx, the sixth carnelian, the seventh chrysolite, the eighth beryl, the ninth topaz, the tenth chrysoprase, the eleventh jacinth, and the twelfth amethyst. [21]The twelve gates were twelve pearls, each gate made of a single pearl. The street of the city was of pure gold, like transparent glass.

[22]I did not see a temple in the city, because the Lord God Almighty and the Lamb are its temple. [23]The city does not need the sun or the moon to shine on it, for the glory of God gives it light, and the Lamb is its lamp. [24]The nations will walk by its light, and the kings of the earth will bring their splendor into it. [25]On no day will its gates ever be shut, for there will be no night there. [26]The glory and honor of the nations will be brought into it. [27]Nothing impure will ever enter it, nor will anyone who does what is shameful or deceitful, but only those whose names are written in the Lamb's book of life.

John's vision of the new Jerusalem expands on what he had first seen in this vision of heaven (verse 2). The angel with the seven bowls (see 17:1) invited him to see "the bride, the wife of the Lamb" (verse 9). The same angel who announced the destruction of the church's enemies shows him the church's final glory.

Paul told the Corinthians that through faith they became the bride of Christ: "I promised you to one husband, to Christ, so that I might present you as a pure virgin to him" (2 Corinthians 11:2). In this world members of Christ's church, his bride, lapse in faithfulness to their vows, but Jesus will honor his promise as a bridegroom. In heaven we will be "the wife of the Lamb" (verse 9).

The angel carried John away in spirit (verse 10; see 1:10; 4:2). A mountain peak provided a vantage point where John could view the magnificent new Jerusalem descending from heaven. The holy city came "down out of heaven" (verse 10), where it was prepared. It came "from God" (verse 10) who readied it for his bride.

The city "shone with the glory of God" (verse 11). When Israel finished setting up the tabernacle in the wilderness, "the glory of the LORD filled [it]" (Exodus 40:34). Again, when the ark was brought to Solomon's temple, "the glory of the LORD filled his temple" (1 Kings 8:11). The appearance of the glory of the Lord was a special way in which God displayed his promise to be with his people. God's full glory will shine through his church like a resplendent jewel.

The physical description of the new Jerusalem begins in verse 12. It is highly figurative, using pictures from the Old Testament tabernacle and Solomon's temple. John is not describing an actual city, but the bride of Christ in heaven. The beauty and symmetry of the dimensions are not to be understood literally. They are meant to paint a picture of the safety, beauty, and perfection of the saints in glory.

The features and the measurements of the temple all number 12 or a multiple of 12. John has used the number 12 before to denote the church (see 4:4; 7:4). The city wall has 12 gates with an angel posted to guard each gate (verse 12). The walls and the angels symbolize the protection God's people enjoy in his presence. "Nothing impure will ever enter it, nor will anyone who does what is shameful or deceitful" (verse 27). The names of the 12 tribes of Israel written on the gates remind any who would enter that only God's spiritual

Israel, members of his church, may enter. The three gates on each side (verse 13) recall that God's spiritual Israel is gathered from the four corners of the earth (see 7:9).

The foundation of the city draws a New Testament picture of the church. The city wall had 12 foundations, each with the name of an apostle on it. Paul told the Ephesians that they were "fellow citizens with God's people and members of God's household, built on the foundation of the apostles and prophets" (Ephesians 2:19,20). Just as the 24 elders on the thrones represented all believers (see 4:4), the 12 tribes of Israel represent the Old Testament church and the 12 apostles, the New Testament church. Yet in heaven all are built into the same church.

The angel who took John up the high mountain to see the city now reveals a golden "measuring rod" to measure the city (verse 15). Like the Holy of Holies in Solomon's temple (2 Chronicles 3:8), the holy city was laid out in a perfect cube (verse 16). But while the holy place of the temple was 30 feet square, the new Jerusalem was infinitely larger, about 1,400 miles on each side and 1,400 miles high. The immense size of the city easily accommodates the "great multitude in heaven" (19:1). Its cubical shape reminds us that all the saints for all eternity enjoy the special presence of God's glory, once reserved only for the Holy of Holies.

The wall was 144 cubits, or 215 feet, thick (verse 17). It might be hard to imagine how a wall 1,400 miles high could be built only two hundred feet thick, but John is not presenting engineer's plans. With the wall made of jasper, he is portraying the beauty and safety the elect will enjoy in the presence of God. The same must be said about the precious stones that decorate the foundations (verses 19, 20). It is not possible for us to identify all these stones with certainty, but that is not important. The precious jewels, the pearly gates, and the translucent gold streets are not what heaven is really made of. All symbolically radiate with the light of God's glory in the center of the city. All are earthly symbols of what it will be like to be a member of the church in God's eternal presence.

What being in the presence of God will be like is pictured another way in the next three verses. John is a little surprised that he did not see a temple in the city. The tabernacle, the temple, or some building for public worship is the center of the believer's attention throughout this life. The glory of the Lord, the ark of the covenant, and the Holy of Holies were the focal point of God's presence in the Old Testament. In the New Testament, Jesus promised his presence wherever believers gather: "For where two or three come together, there am I with them" (Matthew 18:20). But in heaven, "the old order of things has passed away" (verse 4). No buildings or signs are needed to mark God's presence and to offer his grace. Heaven is the perfect fulfillment of earthly worship.

No temples or church buildings are needed in heaven "because the Lord God Almighty and the Lamb are its temple" (verse 22). What we on earth receive intermittently through Word and sacrament, we will enjoy perpetually in heaven in God's presence. We will bask in God's amazing grace. In John's vision God's grace is illustrated by light. "The city does not need the sun or the moon to shine on it, for the glory of God gives it light, and the Lamb is its lamp" (verse 23). God's glory derives from many attributes, such as power, justice, and wisdom. But his greatest glory is the undeserved love he displayed through the Lamb. Thus the two phrases "the glory of God gives it light" and "the Lamb is its lamp" explain each other. They mean the same thing. The Lamb is the glory of God, and the glorious love God showed poor sinners by sending his Son will illuminate the saints forever.

All who embraced this grace on earth will benefit from its light in heaven. "The nations will walk by its light, and the kings of the earth will bring their splendor into it" (verse 24). Isaiah's prophecy of the coming Savior will be fulfilled: "So will he sprinkle many nations, and kings will shut their mouths because of him" (Isaiah 52:15). The word "nations" represents the diverse and universal outreach of Jesus' gospel. "Repentance and forgiveness of sins will be preached in his name to all nations" (Luke 24:47). Included among the saints will be some of the nations' rulers who espoused and championed the gospel of grace. The "splendor" of kings (verse 24) and the "glory and honor of the nations" (verse 26) that are brought into heaven will submit to the greater glory of God. "All kings will bow down to him and all nations will serve him" (Psalm 72:11).

In connection with the eternal light of heaven, John mentions the gates again in verse 25 (see verses 12,13). The symbolic nature of the gates is illustrated by the fact that they will never be shut (verse 25). The gates represent the perfect safety the saints enjoy in heaven. Nothing will ever harm those who live eternally in the light of God's glory. There is no night, no evil lurking in the shadows. The Lamb has defeated all our enemies; there is no need to lock the gates.

The peace and safety of heaven derive from its purity and holiness. John alludes to Old Testament ceremonial law to illustrate this. "Nothing impure" (verse 27) means nothing that was ceremonially unclean for Israel. The word *unclean* occurs more than one hundred times in Leviticus. God's people were to separate themselves from people and things that God designated as impure. With those ceremonial laws God taught his people that they were under his special protection, set apart for him by his covenant of grace. Those laws were fulfilled by Jesus when he lived a life of perfection. An imperfect world keeps us from the full enjoyment of Jesus' holiness and safety. But the gates of heaven will welcome "those whose names are written in the Lamb's book of life" (verse 27) to a full and permanent appreciation of what it means to be God's special people.

The river of life

22 **Then the angel showed me the river of the water of life, as clear as crystal, flowing from the throne of God and of the Lamb ²down the middle of the great street of the city. On each side of the river stood the tree of life, bearing twelve crops of fruit, yielding its fruit every month. And the leaves of the tree are for the healing of the nations. ³No longer will there be any curse. The throne of God and of the Lamb will be in the city, and his servants will serve him. ⁴They will see his face, and his name will be on their foreheads. ⁵There will be no more night. They will not need the light of a lamp or the light of the sun, for the Lord God will give them light. And they will reign for ever and ever.**

The angel who led John to see the new heaven and earth (21:3), brought him to a high mountain to view the new Jerusalem (21:9,10), and measured the holy city (21:15) now shows him "the river of the water of life" (verse 1). "On each side of the river stood the tree of life" (verse 2). The scene is similar, but not identical, to the Garden of Eden.

In Eden there were two special trees, the tree of life and the tree of the knowledge of good and evil (Genesis 2:9). Adam and Eve sinned when they ate of the tree of the knowledge of good and evil. In heaven John sees only one tree, the tree of life, growing on both sides of the river. In heaven we are confirmed in holiness; we cannot sin so we cannot die.

As the tree of life grows from both sides of the river, eternal life grows forever from grace. At Eden God placed "cherubim and a flaming sword flashing back and forth to guard the way to the tree of life" (Genesis 3:24). But in heaven we will again have access to this tree.

Heaven will perfectly restore the paradise we lost through the sin of Adam and Eve. God cursed the earth because of Adam's sin, and "the LORD God banished him from the Garden of Eden" (Genesis 3:23). But now the river of life flows down the middle of the holy city from the throne of God and the Lamb. Saints will be sustained by the never-ending flow of God's grace.

The tree of life produces 12 crops of fruit, one crop each month. The number is obviously symbolic since day and night, years and seasons are gone. The number 12 is the number of the church (see 21:12,13). The 12 crops signify that the church in glory will be nurtured by the tree of life that grows from the river of God's grace. Ezekiel prophesied that fruit trees would grow from a river flowing from the temple: "Their fruit will serve for food and their leaves for healing" (Ezekiel 47:12). So the tree of life will provide "healing of the nations" (verse 2). All the suffering caused by Adam's fall will be ended. "No longer will there be any curse" (verse 3).

What will we do in heaven? John says, "The throne of God and of the Lamb will be in the city, and his servants will serve him" (verse 3). Those who imagine heaven as a place of idleness and boredom are mistaken. Besides singing songs of praise, our time in heaven will be spent serving God and the Lamb. We don't know exactly what that service will be. Because our service is mentioned in connection with the throne, it will include reigning with God. "They will reign for ever and ever" (verse 5). Given what we do know about heaven—its perfection, its beauty, its lack of sorrow, and God's presence there—we can be sure that our service will be pure pleasure.

At the beginning of his Gospel, John wrote, "No one has ever seen God, but God the One and Only, who is at the Father's side, has made him known" (John 1:18). During our life on earth, we enjoy God's presence, but sin keeps us from seeing God face to face. The sinful nature remains also in believers, so God must veil his direct presence from them, even from great men like Moses (Exodus 3:5,6; 33:18-23). Yet all Christians have the sure hope they will see God someday. David prayed, "You have made known to me the path of life; you will fill me with joy in your presence, with eternal pleasures at your right hand" (Psalm 16:11). Paul wrote, "For we know in part and we prophesy in part, but when perfection comes, the imperfect disappears. Now we see but a poor reflection as in a mirror; then we shall see face to face. Now I know in part; then I shall know fully, even as I am fully known" (1 Corinthians 13:9,10,12). "We know that when he appears, we shall be like him, for we shall see him as he is" (1 John 3:2).

The pleasure of seeing God face to face will come in heaven. John writes, "They will see his face, and his name will be on their foreheads" (verse 4). Seeing God face to face and wearing his name are closely connected. Sin prevents us from looking at God. But when Jeremiah promised the Messiah, he said that would change: "In those days Judah will be saved and Jerusalem will live in safety. This is the name by which it will be called: The LORD Our Righteousness" (Jeremiah 33:16). When we die in faith, our sinful nature dies and we are raised in righteousness to wear our Savior's name. This is the promise Jesus makes to those who overcome: "I will write on him the name of my God and the name of the city of my God, the new Jerusalem, which is coming down out of heaven from my God; and I will also write on him my new name" (3:12).

Again John mentions the light of God in heaven. He already explained that "the glory of God gives it light, and the Lamb is its lamp" (21:23). Now he talks about the effect the glory of God will have on life in heaven. The light of God's glory means that there won't be artificial or created lights in heaven: "They will not need the light of a lamp or the light of the sun" (verse 5). It also means that time will not be measured by the turning of the sun because "there will be no more night" (verse 5).

Heaven is a place of beauty, safety, perfection, and eternal life. The source and center of all this is the glory of God's grace that lights up the holy city.

CONCLUSION
(22:6-21)

John and the angel

⁶The angel said to me, "These words are trustworthy and true. The Lord, the God of the spirits of the prophets, sent his angel to show his servants the things that must soon take place."

⁷"Behold, I am coming soon! Blessed is he who keeps the words of the prophecy in this book."

⁸I, John, am the one who heard and saw these things. And when I had heard and seen them, I fell down to worship at the feet of the angel who had been showing them to me. ⁹But he said to me, "Do not do it! I am a fellow servant with you and with your brothers the prophets and of all who keep the words of this book. Worship God!"

¹⁰Then he told me, "Do not seal up the words of the prophecy of this book, because the time is near. ¹¹Let him who does wrong continue to do wrong; let him who is vile continue to be vile; let him who does right continue to do right; and let him who is holy continue to be holy."

The seven visions are over, but the angel who showed John the last magnificent vision of the holy city has two more important messages for John to bring to his readers. First, John is to communicate the divine nature of what he has just seen and written. "The angel said to me, 'These words are trustworthy and true'" (verse 6). Jesus spoke these same words before from the throne in the new Jerusalem (21:5). John did not dream up the Revelation. This book is not a compilation of self-pitying reveries of an exile on the island of Patmos.

It is remarkable that this same phrase, "trustworthy and true"—used twice to describe the words of the Revelation—is also used twice to describe Jesus himself. When ascribed to Jesus, the NIV translates this phrase differently: "faithful and true" (3:14; 19:11). But John used identical Greek words for Jesus and his Word. In his Gospel John also closely associated Jesus with the Word. He wrote that at Jesus' birth the Word of God became incarnate: "The Word became flesh and made his dwelling among us" (John 1:14). Jesus explained what we are to understand from this: "You diligently study the Scriptures because you think that by them you possess eternal life. These are the Scriptures that testify about me" (John 5:39).

What John recorded in the Revelation came from God and from Jesus. The angel said, "The Lord, the God of the spirits of the prophets, sent his angel" (verse 6). Later we read, "I, Jesus, have sent my angel" (verse 16). Jesus and the God of the prophets are one in essence. As they share the throne in heaven (verse 1), they share in the work of putting their divine message into the hearts of the prophets.

Earlier, John referred to the Holy Spirit as "the seven spirits" (1:4; 3:1; 4:5; 5:6), and all John's references to the Holy Spirit are in the plural at the beginning of the book. By contrast, in this last chapter he refers to the Holy Spirit in the singular, "the Spirit" (verse 17). For that reason we understand "the spirits of the prophets" (verse 6) to refer not to the Holy Spirit but to the soul and personality of the Bible's penmen. The Lord God ruled and guided John's spirit in the same way he led all the inspired prophets.

The doctrine of divine inspiration is not a jewel to be stored on the back shelves of theological libraries. It is a practical teaching that impresses believers with the urgency of applying the Bible to their daily lives.

The reason God sent his angel to John was "to show his servants the things that must soon take place" (verse 6). The Revelation is relevant. It portrays what is happening in the world today and what will soon happen.

Twice Jesus interjects his voice into the angel's conversation with John to say how urgent is our need to apply the words of the Revelation. "Behold, I am coming soon!" Jesus says (verse 7). Although the angel was speaking in the previous verse and Jesus does not identify himself, we know he is the one speaking here. Later, Jesus will break in again with the same words and identify himself as "the Alpha and the Omega" (verse 13).

All that John wrote in Revelation is bracketed by Jesus' promises of blessing to those who read the book. The first blessing comes at the beginning (1:3), and the last occurs here: "Blessed is he who keeps the words of the prophecy in this book" (verse 7). Jesus will return as a thief in the night. Death comes upon us unaware. A person's regret over not reading the Bible while he or she had the chance will not win God's heart at the last judgment. It will only add to the agony of going into eternity unprepared. But blessing—the greatest blessing of all—comes to those who learn of Jesus from his Word.

John identifies himself at the beginning (1:1,2) and at the end (verse 8) as the author of Revelation. John did not invent the contents of this book. He only recorded what he had heard and seen (verse 8) from the angel "who had been showing them to [him]" (verse 8). God inspired his prophets and apostles with such marvelous truths that they tried to ward off their readers' natural tendency to doubt what they wrote. Peter argued, "We did not follow cleverly invented stories when we told you about the power and coming of our Lord Jesus Christ, but we were eyewitnesses of his majesty"

(2 Peter 1:16). Paul also attested to the fact of the resurrection by citing eyewitnesses (1 Corinthians 15:1-11).

John was so overwhelmed by what he had seen and heard that he fell at the foot of the angel to worship him (verse 8). Perhaps since Jesus had interjected his word of blessing, John mistook the angel to be the Lord. But the angel stopped him: "Do not do it!" (verse 9). The angel placed himself on the same level as John: "I am a fellow servant with you" (verse 9). Angels and men alike are creatures of God. Worshiping angels detracts from the glory of our Creator and Savior. Paul said that those who worship angels have "lost connection with the Head" (Colossians 2:19).

God assigns his creatures different roles in relationship to one another. But in respect to God, all—angels, prophets, and "all who keep the words of this book" (verse 9)—are brothers. All are fellow servants. In heaven "his servants will serve him" (verse 3) with a perfect understanding of their role. On earth we respect each other for the area of service God assigns us, but on earth and in heaven we give only to our Creator and Savior the glory that belongs to him: "Worship God!" (verse 9).

The angel repeats the twin themes of Jesus' imminent return and the need for attention to the Scriptures: "Do not seal up the words of the prophecy of this book because the time is near" (verse 10; see also verse 7). Earlier, John was told to "seal up" (10:4) what the seven thunders said. Now he is told not to seal up the words of the Revelation he received. The Bible was written for our salvation, not our curiosity. God withholds some things from us for our good, but we trust that what he has written in the Bible "is useful for teaching" (2 Timothy 3:16). Much of what Jesus did on earth was not recorded in John's Gospel either (John 20:30). But what he did write was "written that you may believe that Jesus is the

Christ, the Son of God, and that by believing you may have life in his name" (John 20:31). What we do not find in Revelation must not keep us from the rich treasures it does contain.

Verse 11 poses the consequences for those who gave their attention to the Bible and those who did not. The angel is not suggesting that those who neglect Scriptures should remain in their unbelief. Such a wish would not reflect the will of God, "who wants all men to be saved and to come to a knowledge of the truth" (1 Timothy 2:4). The angel has just warned, "the time is near" (verse 10). The setting for verse 11 is after the time has come. The time of grace for reading the Scriptures and learning of Jesus is over.

When death or judgment day marks the end of our time of grace, it is too late to give attention to God's Word. "Man is destined to die once, and after that to face judgment" (Hebrews 9:27). What we are at the time of death or judgment is what we always will be. Change and regret will not alter our eternal fate. Jesus said, "There is a judge for the one who rejects me and does not accept my words; that very word which I spoke will condemn him at the last day" (John 12:48). Our final relationship to Jesus' Word is the relationship we will always have to it. What a compelling warning this is for those who despise the means of grace and what an encouragement for those who love God's Word!

Jesus and John

¹²"Behold, I am coming soon! My reward is with me, and I will give to everyone according to what he has done. ¹³I am the Alpha and the Omega, the First and the Last, the Beginning and the End.

¹⁴"Blessed are those who wash their robes, that they may have the right to the tree of life and may go through the gates into the city. ¹⁵Outside are the dogs, those who practice magic

arts, the sexually immoral, the murderers, the idolaters and everyone who loves and practices falsehood.

¹⁶"I, Jesus, have sent my angel to give you this testimony for the churches. I am the Root and the Offspring of David, and the bright Morning Star."

¹⁷The Spirit and the bride say, "Come!" And let him who hears say, "Come!" Whoever is thirsty, let him come; and whoever wishes, let him take the free gift of the water of life.

¹⁸I warn everyone who hears the words of the prophecy of this book: If anyone adds anything to them, God will add to him the plagues described in this book. ¹⁹And if anyone takes words away from this book of prophecy, God will take away from him his share in the tree of life and in the holy city, which are described in this book.

As he did in verse 7, Jesus also interjects his words of comfort for the suffering church here: "Behold, I am coming soon!" (verse 12). These words always have a double edge, warning the unrepentant and comforting the faithful. Still, they are spoken here primarily to comfort those who find it hard to hold on to their faith in a wicked world. Jesus will return in victory and fulfill all the wonderful promises of glory for his suffering church.

This time Jesus identifies himself: "I am the Alpha and the Omega" (verse 13). Alpha and omega are the first and last letters of the Greek alphabet. Jesus uses this name to say that he is the eternal, changeless God (see 1:17,18). This name assures his readers that he will keep his promises. "My reward is with me, and I will give to everyone according to what he has done" (verse 12). He will come as he promised. He will bring with him all the rewards he promised to give to those who overcome: "the tree of life" (2:7), "the crown of life" (2:10), "a new name" (2:17), "authority over the nations" (2:26), their names in the "book of life" (3:5), "the name of the city of my God" (3:12), and "the right to sit with me on my throne" (3:21).

Jesus will reward everyone "according to what he has done" (verse 12). This does not mean that salvation is by works. Jesus used language like this in his parable of the sheep and the goats (Matthew 25:31-46). On the Last Day Jesus will point to our good works to demonstrate the faith we held in our hearts. We will be judged worthy of our reward on the basis of the white clothes Jesus gives us (see 19:8). But since "faith without deeds is dead" (James 2:26), the good works of believers will prove that they "have not soiled their clothes" (3:4).

Jesus leaves no doubt that this is how we are to understand the basis for his final judgment. He says, "Blessed are those who wash their robes, that they may have the right to the tree of life" (verse 14). The "filthy rags" (Isaiah 64:6) of our own righteousness are gone. Believers "have washed their robes and made them white in the blood of the Lamb" (7:14). Not what they have done but what Jesus did for them gives them the right to the tree of life (see 22:2,3) and access to the holy city (see 21:25-27).

The blessing in verse 14 is the seventh and last word of blessing in Revelation. The number 7 symbolizes the loving action of the three persons of God toward those who inhabit the four corners of the earth. This last blessing incorporates everything promised by the six that preceded it. This seventh blessing promises that God will be united with man in the highest sense. The seventh blessing is heaven.

Not everyone, though, receives this ultimate blessing. For the third time since the vision of the holy city, we read a detailed list of those who will be excluded from heaven. Common to all three lists are those who tell lies: "liars" (21:8); "deceitful" (21:27); and "everyone who loves and practices falsehood" (verse 15). Jesus said Satan's approach is characterized by "not holding to the truth" (John 8:44). To reject the truth about Jesus is the ultimate lie. The lives of unbelievers to some extent are characterized by this self-deceit.

To the Jews "dogs" meant the Gentiles, those who were excluded from God's chosen people (see Matthew 15:26). In Philippians 3:2, Paul used the term in a more general way to mean unbelievers ("Watch out for those dogs, those men who do evil"). That is how John used the term here. The list of coarse sinners that follows his mention of dogs explains who is included by the term. Everyone whose life belies the gospel of Jesus Christ is excluded from God's chosen people.

Again Jesus identifies himself. His reason for doing so is to encourage the churches to receive the Revelation as his own words. He sent his angel. This is his testimony to the churches. He uses names that the churches would associate with their Savior: "the Root and the Offspring of David, and the bright Morning Star" (verse 16). Through Jesus "all things were made" (John 1:3). Thus Jesus was David's Creator, his root, or source. But when Jesus became human, he was born as a descendant, or offspring, of the same David. John's readers must identify the one speaking as the Messiah, God's Son and David's son. Like a bright morning star heralds the coming of a new day, Jesus promises a new heaven and a new earth where "the Lamb is its lamp" (21:23).

Sinners should not read Revelation's severe words of warning as anything but the loving concern of a gracious God calling them to repentance. In this closing section John has credited his words to God (verse 6), to Jesus (verse 16), and to the angel who showed him the vision of heaven (verse 8).

To their words John now adds another invitation: "The Spirit and the bride say, 'Come!'" (verse 17). The Spirit is the Holy Spirit. The bride is the bride of Christ, the members of his church (see 19:7). The invitation is intended for those who do not yet believe in Jesus. "Come!" means leave your sins and come to Jesus in faith. Everyone who hears Revelation's loving invitation with the ears of faith will join in to invite still others: "Come!" This is one of the great evangelical calls of Scripture. It shines with God's universal love for sinful people. No one is excluded from the invitation. It reminds us that the dire warnings of this book do not exclude anyone from the forgiveness earned by Jesus. It assures us that the gospel of Jesus Christ excludes no one. Those who are barred from heaven exclude themselves by refusing to hear and believe.

Jesus and his church welcome "whoever is thirsty," (verse 17), that is, everyone whose sins make him thirsty for forgiveness. This invitation parallels Isaiah's: "Come, all you who are thirsty, come to the waters; and you who have no money, come . . . buy . . . without money and without cost" (Isaiah 55:1). The hymnwriter beautifully described the receiving hand of faith when he wrote, "Nothing in my hand I bring, simply to thy cross I cling" (CW 389:3). When the inviting Spirit moves him, anyone who wishes can "take the free gift of the water of life" (verse 17). The word order of the original Greek is similar to our English way of speaking: "Take the water of life—*gratis!*" It's free! There is no charge. Salvation is by grace alone.

The warnings and promises of Revelation are critical to the eternal destiny of souls. That is why John warns against changing even one word. Moses warned Israel about God's law in the same way: "Do not add to what I command you and do not subtract from it, but keep the commands of the

LORD your God that I give you" (Deuteronomy 4:2). John's warning, of course, applies to how we handle all Scripture. We seek to share God's warnings and promises in a way that "correctly handles the word of truth" (2 Timothy 2:15). Teachers who soft-pedal the threats of God's law or trade away God's promises of eternal salvation for temporal social benefits fall under the curse of this warning.

Last word to the churches

[20]He who testifies to these things says, "Yes, I am coming soon." Amen. Come, Lord Jesus. [21]The grace of the Lord Jesus be with God's people. Amen.

Through John's pen Jesus promises those who contend for the faith that he will return quickly. This is our Lord's answer to the souls of the martyrs who cry out from heaven, "How long, Sovereign Lord . . . ?" (6:10). Like Jesus' discouraged disciples, we also are often tempted to ask, "What does he mean by 'a little while'?" (John 16:18). Our Lord's answer is simple: "I am coming soon" (verse 20).

By its promises of sure victory for the saints, Revelation offers a perspective from which believers view their daily struggles. Jesus' promises create faith; faith produces patience. Such patience views spiritual trials as Paul did: "For our light and momentary troubles are achieving for us an eternal glory that far outweighs them all" (2 Corinthians 4:17). "I consider that our present sufferings are not worth comparing with the glory that will be revealed in us" (Romans 8:18). This is the perspective we gain when we read and believe the Revelation of Jesus Christ to John. For this blessing we join John and pray, "Amen. Come, Lord Jesus."

John closes his letter with his desire that his readers continue to live in "the grace of the Lord Jesus" (verse 21).

"Yes, I am coming soon." (22:20)